MW00489743

HOPE FOR ETHIOPIA

DESTA HELISO

ICCS
PRESS

iccspress.com

Copyright © 2021 by ICCS Press, Inc.

Published by ICCS Press, 616 Prospect Street, New Haven, CT 06511
www.iccspress.com

All rights reserved. No part of this book may be reproduced in any form or by
any electronic or mechanical means, including information storage and retrieval
systems, without written permission from ICCS Press, except for the use of
brief quotations in a book review.

Artwork: Mekdes Zeleke Kabeto

Cover Design: speersdesign.com

ISBN:978-1-62428-016-0; 978-1-62428-019-1 (EPUB).

Printed in the United States of America on acid-free paper.

In memory of Peter Cotterell (1930-2021), my enabler and mentor, who was happy to be called white Habesha and whose little book Cry Ethiopia continues to inspire me.

CONTENTS

ACKNOWLEDGMENTS

I am indebted to many for the completion of this book. I cannot mention all the names here, but I would like to thank especially Roberta and Howard Ahmanson and Steven Ferguson for their support and encouragement. Steven was the one who first challenged me to express my hope for Ethiopia.

I am grateful to Meagan Clark for proofreading the final draft. Michael Glerup made it possible for this book to be published, marketed and distributed. I cannot sufficiently express the depth of my gratitude to him.

I thank my family: my wife, Jo Jeffery, for her support and corrective and critical comments on the manuscript; and my children for their love and patience.

Finally, I thank the God of hope, who continues to fill me with joy and peace and whose grace enables me to hope even in the face of the most hopeless of situations.

Desta Heliso

PREFACE

A few years ago, I was challenged by a friend to write a short book to introduce a non-Ethiopian audience to a voice of hope for Ethiopia. I accepted the challenge, but I was under no illusion that expressing hope in the most fluid, uncertain, and often, most hopeless situations would be easy. Despite the delay in its fruition for various reasons, I am glad the idea eventually materialized.

Some view hope as wishful thinking, mere desire, or as the Roman historian Cicero said, "poor man's bread." However, it seems universally accepted that human creatures cannot live without hope. To be sure, hope is painful, because what we hope for is invisible and immediately unreachable, but there is no question that along with faith and love, hope is foundational for human existence.

The writer of the letter to the Hebrews in the Bible equates hope with what we do not see. For the writer, it is faith that enables us to be sure of what we hope for and be certain of what we do not see. Ethiopians have held onto this belief for centuries. They have learned that to hope in the face of even the most fluid, uncertain and hopeless of situations is worth it.

Gordon Brown, the former prime minister of the United Kingdom, recounts a story in the preface of his memoir, *My Life, Our Times*, about an official loan of a painting he offered to Barack Obama during his first visit to London in 2009 as U.S. president. The painting, which belonged to the Government Art Collection, is called *Hope*, which was created by the British artist George Frederic Watts. It was this painting that inspired Barack Obama's book *The Audacity of Hope*. The painting was about a blindfolded girl sitting on a globe and trying to play a lyre, which has all its strings broken except one. She tries to listen to the faint music by bending her head. The atmosphere is one of sadness and hopelessness, but Brown rightly says that the painting reflects the idea that "even in the most hopeless of situations we can, and must, seek grounds for hope." That is why Obama also said: "[Hope] in the face of difficulty. Hope in the face of uncertainty. The audacity of hope. In the end, that is God's greatest gift to us... A belief in things not seen. A belief that there are better days ahead."

Both Brown and Obama believe that politics can deliver a message of hope if it embodies ideas that are built on a foundation of hope. Ethiopia's hope, too, lies in a sound political system capable of creating a better future for Ethiopia and its citizens. But it goes further than that. Ethiopia is an old nation that has experienced multiple conflicts, famines, and political upheavals over the last half-century alone. Aid, loans, and ideologies may have helped Ethiopia, but they have not addressed underlying problems. Ethiopia remains a country whose beauties and wonders are often overshadowed by its tragedies and uncertainties, sadness and hopelessness.

Ethiopia's hope for a better future lies in its transformed citizens and recalibrated socio-economic, cultural and religious values and practices. This is what I seek to express in this small book, because I, too, have the audacity to hope and believe, as Martin Luther King Jr. said, that people everywhere, including Ethiopians, "can have three meals a day for their bodies, education and culture for their minds, and dignity, equality and freedom for their spirits."

My expression of hope for Ethiopia is also my expression of hope for Africa. Ethiopia is central in the life of Africa, not least because it played a significant role in the establishment of the *Organization of African Unity*, which is now called the *African Union*, whose headquarters are in Addis Ababa. However, it has taken many Ethiopians a little longer to claim Africa! Now Ethiopians, including myself, are claiming Africa as much as Africans have claimed Ethiopia probably for centuries. In my journey of appreciating my African heritage, my involvement with the *Association for Christian Theological Education in Africa* played some part. But it was the late Tom Oden's challenge to us Africans to consider early African Christianity's contribution to the world that played a decisive role.

Getting to know the late Lamin Sanneh and his works and being part of his *Church and Society Workshops* also provided me with new perspectives about ethnicity, citizenship, and religion in Africa. Some of Lamin's ideas and dreams for Africa feature in different sections in this book, albeit in a fragmented manner. His sudden death was a considerable loss for Africa and the world. We, Africans in particular, sorely miss his intellectual example about what is possible and his personal encouragement for us to keep going despite all the challenges faced in Africa. When I last saw him in November 2018 during my visit to New Haven, as we said goodbye to each other, he said to me, "keep the flag flying high." He certainly kept the flag flying high until his death, as a scholar and a human being, whose Christian convictions shaped his thinking and living and whose hope for a better Africa never died.

INTRODUCTION

Ethiopia is a country blessed with natural beauty and incredible ethnic and ecological diversity, but it is a victim of countless misfortunes. Staggering numbers of droughts, locust swarms, famines, diseases, and plagues have repeatedly devastated livestock, human lives, and the ecosystem. There have been times when the situation has been very bleak. Towards the end of the 19th century, for example, Ethiopia experienced a great famine, which was accompanied by diseases such as cholera, typhus, and smallpox. It decimated a third of the entire population. In the 20th century too, in the 1970s, 80s, and 90s in particular, the country experienced significant droughts and famines, which took the lives of millions of people.[1]

Ethiopia's tragic misfortunes may be attributed to unpredictable climate, rainfall variability, cultivation methods, overgrazing, deforestation, and poor land management. But they can also be attributed to destructive political ideologies, ineffective governance, economic strategies, corruption, religious

failures, lack of education, harmful cultural values, and traditional practices, and ethnocentrism. In 1988, Dr. Peter
Cotterell attributed Ethiopia's problems to deforestation, a
lost generation due to famine, brain drain and political
killings, the cost of arms, Marxist domination, foreign aid
policies, and lack of political will.[2] Of course, much has
changed since the 1980s. Today Ethiopia's problems have
taken different and even more dangerous shapes and forms.
However we understand Ethiopia's issues and their root
causes, the unceasing human suffering makes one wonder if
Ethiopia is not a hopeless country led by ineffective political
and religious leaders.

Ethiopia's neighboring countries such as Yemen, Somalia,
and South Sudan continue to experience similar disasters and
intractable socio-political turmoil. In that sense, Ethiopia's
problems are not unique. However, given the country's historical position, human and economic potential, the magnitude
and recurrence of its issues, human contributions to them, and
the consistent lack of sustainable solutions, Ethiopia's situation
is puzzlingly unique. To be sure, according to the human development index, Ethiopia has clearly shown improvements over
the last few decades. People are healthier and living longer, and
the standards of living and education are improving.

Some specific examples of progress on the socio-political
and economic fronts are freedom of religion, growth in university education opportunities, significant infrastructural development (roads, railways, and bridges), expanding manufacturing
industry, and multiple mega-dam construction projects to
generate hydro-electric power. We have also seen the emer-
gence of a flourishing hotel and tourism sector, banking industry, and a rapidly growing, well-managed and world-class airline

industry. Until recently, the country has enjoyed rapid economic growth and an expanding middle class.

However, these signs of progress have enabled many Ethiopians to cope and hope has been overshadowed by complex political, economic, administrative, and inter-ethnic problems. The present situation is consistent with Ethiopia's historical journey, characterized by one step forward and two (or even three) steps back. This was the case starting from the early periods, when disparate kingdoms under chiefs and sultans were in existence, to the early 14th century, when Muslim principalities in the southeast became reluctant subjects to the Christian kingdom in the north. It was also the case between the 16th and late 19th centuries when nation formation was set in motion but was hampered by successive devastating battles waged by different groups with political, religious, economic, and ethnocentric-expansionist goals.

As a result, Axum, Harar, Lalibela, and Gonder— some of the cities where progress and human flourishing itself began— failed to keep developing. This became even more stark in the 20th century. Ample opportunities were squandered during the era of Emperor Haile-Selassie (1930-1974). Any progress made was almost completely wiped out by the military-communist regime that governed from 1974 to 1991.

During the Ethiopian People's Revolutionary Democratic Front (EPRDF) era from 1991 to 2018, dangerous trends developed. Most common were: ethnocentric political arrangements and the resulting inter-ethnic tensions and marginalization of minority groups; endemic corruption; maladministration; land-grabbing in the name of investment; curtailed freedom of expression; tightly controlled media; lack of free and fair elections; the absence of a level playing field in politics and business; a politically driven educational system; and constitutionally determined threats for the integrity of Ethiopia as a nation-state. As a result, the country was on the verge of a civil war between 2016 and 2018. That was averted as a result of a smooth power transfer within the ruling party (EPRDF), for which the then Prime Minister, Mr. Hailemariam Desalegn, is to be commended. After the power transfer and Dr. Abiy Ahmed became Prime Minister in April 2018, hope swept through the country.

There were good reasons for the people to be hopeful. Love, forgiveness, peace, and unity became central in political discourse. Sweeping and staggering reforms were initiated. Political prisoners were released. Death sentences passed on politically motivated grounds were reversed. The state of emergency was lifted. Freedom of the press was declared. Banned and blocked media outlets were allowed to operate freely. Religious factions within the Ethiopian Orthodox Tewahido Church (EOTC) and Islam declared a truce. The political landscape widened with opposition parties no longer regarded as enemies or anti-peace forces. Judicial and security institutions were declared to be independent of political influence. Armed groups ceased hostilities and moved back into Ethiopia peacefully. Reforms were introduced in the economic sector. A peace agreement with Eritrea was signed, following which borders between the two nations opened, and Ethiopian Airlines resumed its flights to Asmara after 20 long years. However, huge threats and concerns remained. In fact, the situation at the moment is much more volatile than when the power transfer happened.

BACKGROUND OF ETHIOPIA'S
RECURRING PROBLEMS

Ethiopia's recurring problems are born from historically embedded ethno-political and religious issues that can be explained as follows.

First, Ethiopia's problems are related to the process of state formation. Ethiopia as a state was created from different people groups by promoting ideals believed to unite these groups and help transcend their differences. It may not be possible to establish precisely and agree on exactly when Ethiopia's historical journey as a nation-state began. Still, if we start from the turn of the first millennium when Axum was a powerful kingdom, we know that disparate kingdoms became reluctant subjects to the Christian kingdom in the north. Then from the 14th to late 19th centuries, the process of theologically legitimated nation-state formation was set in motion, motivated not only by advancing the Christian religion but by political dominance that was believed to facilitate economic benefits. This process of nation-state formation brought about a shared national identity.

However, as the process itself was often coercive, manipulative and bloody, it inevitably left a scar (to a lesser or greater degree) in the psyche of each people group, hence creating what I call a historical volcano. The last theocratic regime tried to keep this historical volcano from constantly erupting by employing shrewd diplomacy, politically arranged marital structures and, more importantly, an inclusive system, which was largely camouflaged by the Amharic language and Orthodox Christianity. The military-communist regime kept this volcano under control by brute force and an insidious focus on the "Mother Land." In both cases, political machinery was devised to suppress existing structures of kinship and multi-layered identities. Such suppression gave rise to ethno-nationalist tendencies and demands for self-determination. This brings me to the second point, which is the Eritrean issue.

Since the Victory of Adwa against the Italians in 1896, following which Eritrea remained an Italian colony, the narrative of Ethiopian-ness was created and recreated, defined and redefined by the political machinery. This machinery was further bolstered after the forces of Fascist Italy were driven out of Ethiopia and Eritrea in 1941, and the latter was under the British protectorate. This was the beginning of trouble for both. After the British rule ended in 1952, the voices that advocated Eritrean independence were overcome by those who favored Eritrea being federated with Ethiopia. This ensured that the Eritrean government was entirely responsible for its internal affairs and the Ethiopian government for the foreign affairs of both Ethiopia and Eritrea. Eritrea now had its own parliament with Tigrigna as its official language and Italian as its second language. This was also the case at schools. But the fateful decision by Emperor Haile-Selassie's government to replace Tigrigna with Amharic and then annex Eritrea as a province of Ethiopia gave birth to an armed resistance that developed into civil war, setting off unending misery and suffering for both Ethiopians and Eritreans to this day.

In connection with this, thirdly, the mushrooming of "liberation movements" is at the root of Ethiopia's problems. While ethnic diversity – characterized by kinship and shared memory, narrative, language and culture of a certain people group – is something that has always been recognized in Ethiopia. It was from the 1960s that ethno-nationalist tendencies started to develop from Ogaden to Eritrea. These ethno-nationalist tendencies developed into liberation movements: Ogaden People's Liberation Front, Oromo People's Liberation Front, Tigrean People's Liberation Front and Eritrean People's Liberation Front are some of the notable examples. The liberation movements referred to the imperialistic, expansionist and oppressive ideology of the Christian kingdom represented by the "Amharas."

In all this, however, there were at least two complicating factors. The first was that the Ethiopian monarchy until 1974 was promoting a policy of national unity symbolised by one flag, one religion, one language, one constitution, and one king. In order to implement this policy, brutal wars were fought between government forces and forces loyal to tribal chiefs. More pertinently, Orthodox Christian governors with their Amharic speaking entourages and security personnel were dispatched to parts of the country under government control and established settlements that later became towns. Indigenous communities mixed with the newcomers, intermarried, and shared their lives and resources together. Another complicating factor, which took place in the 16th century AD, was the violent expansion, conquest, and settlement of the Oromos (an ethnic group native to both Ethiopia and Kenya) with their own language, religion, and leadership structure. They had assimilationist or mass adoption practice, where other people groups voluntarily or involuntarily covenanted themselves to become Oromo, speak the Oromo language, and adopt the Oromo culture. This arguably is an ancient form of 'social engineering', which inevitably had severe demographic consequences. It now means that "liberating one people group" without politically and geographically including the Oromos within that group or any people group within the Oromos would be virtually impossible.

Fourthly, Ethiopia's history of state formation and its religious journey involved both positive interactions and periodic conflicts between Christians and Muslims and the roles of external forces. Several historical and religious factors are in play here. First, radical Islamic elements within Ethiopia and outside have sought to cement the unsubstantiated claim that Ethiopia was part of the "land of Islam" and dream of making Islam both the religion and state in Ethiopia. Second, there are forces that still fuel the flame of fear and hatred by portraying Ethiopian Muslims as the most marginalized group in the Horn of Africa. These forces reject the principle of accommodation in Christian-Muslim relations. Third, as in the early 16th century, there are still jihadist ideals fueled by the theological conviction of forces in the Middle East and the politico-religious ambition of Turkey's President Tayyip Erdogan. Fourth, some Muslim Oromos continue to harbor resentment towards the Ethiopian state because of past suppression and marginalization of Muslim Oromos and coercive attempts to Christianize communities *en masse*. Religious groups in Egypt and Sudan as well as Saudi Arabia have been exploiting this resentment. Fifth, a political vision to turn Ethiopia into a haven of religious tolerance has been difficult to achieve in Ethiopia. The culture of religious intolerance is deeply entrenched in Ethiopia and religious clashes and persecutions continue to occur. Sixth, a Wahhabist form of Islamic extremism has grown in the Horn of Africa, while moderate forms of Sufi Islam and *Al Ahbash* Islam are being weakened.

Finally, at the root of the current problems of Ethiopia are the policies and programs of the Ethiopian People's Revolutionary Democratic Front (EPRDF). Much good has been achieved under the EPRDF, from removal of the oppressive military regime to religious freedom, to relative economic growth, to infrastructural development, to expansion of educational institutions. There is also much that can be regarded as bad. EPRDF's biggest sin is probably its introduction of political and administrative structures along ethnic lines whereby it sought to marry ethnicity with federalism. When this political philosophy failed, leading to civil unrest, the regime simply used brute force to quash dissent.

Some attribute the main reasons for public unrest in 2016-2018 to the dispossession of land rights, the policy of expanding the city of Addis Ababa at the expense of the Oromo farmers, a territorial dispute between the Tigray and Amhara regions, and widespread political repression. These were significant symptoms. The leading cause, in my view, was the federal system built on overemphasis of ethnic diversity, which enabled the interactions between ethnic groups to develop into a "zero-sum game." The emphasis on regional autonomy was excessive, where each region was regarded as sovereign. As a country made up of more than 80 people groups, Ethiopia had 14 provinces in the past. After seizing power in 1991, EPRDF facilitated Eritrea to secede from Ethiopia, which irrevocably changed the integrity of the Ethiopian state system. EPRDF also created a constitutional provision that would enable other people groups to secede from Ethiopia at any time of their choosing. The new ruling party drew new regional borders throughout the country with no regard for minority settlers who had lived in the territories for centuries. This redefinition of Ethiopian boundaries was carried out without any consensual democratic process. It was also characterized by negative territorialism, which led to inter-ethnic clashes and massive internal displacements. The lack of strong institutions and processes that promoted shared rule and national unity means that the new system has taken Ethiopia back to the kind of tribal warfare that existed in the olden days, endangering the country's future as a single nation-state. The absurdity of the new political order cannot be overemphasized, as its disastrous consequences are incalculable.

❧ 2 ❧

PERSONAL STORY

So what hope is there for Ethiopia? This question comes out of my own personal experience. I was born and brought up in the remote malaria-ridden rural South. There I shared a large grass-thatched house with cows, horses, donkeys, sheep, goats, chickens and more than 12 people, including my 8 siblings. I helped my father with farming when it was not school term or when I was not weakened by malaria. We depended on rain and used oxen to plough the land. When droughts and excessive flooding occurred, we had little harvest, so we ran out of grain between July and September and went hungry until we sold some of our livestock to buy food. We had no electricity and no toilet. We used a kerosene lamp to light the house at night and drank brown water from the nearby river. That was half a century ago, and it is still the same for those who live there.

Now, whenever I go back to my home region, I wonder whether there is any hope of progress or what human flourishing for Ethiopia would mean in another half a century. This is not to say that nothing has changed. There are more schools and clinics than before. There is even a tarmacked road that runs from Addis Ababa to our district town, which also has electricity, a bank and a high school. But poverty, ignorance and food insecurity still reign. Inter-ethnic tensions in my home region, for example, have been replicated at clan levels, resulting in inter-clan tensions. EPRDF's ethnocentric political ideology has opened historic wounds and destroyed relationships based on trust and reciprocity. This is part of the story of Ethiopia and Ethiopians as a whole.

Now, as I write these words, a global pandemic caused by Novel Coronavirus Disease (COVID-19) is ravaging the world. While the pandemic has not taken as many lives as projected by epidemiologists, it looks as if it has put Ethiopia two steps backward politically and economically. Also, as I wrote these words, the tension between the Tigray People's Liberation Front (TPLF) and the federal government had grown. None of us knew what the future held, but we lived in hope. My hope was based on Ethiopia's incredible survival in very difficult and dangerous transitions. Ethiopia survived very dangerous transitions from the fragmented rule of the Princes in the 18th century to Emperor Theodros and then to successive emperors, presidents and prime ministers. It also survived two Ethio-Italian wars and very dangerous wars with neighboring nations such as Egypt, Sudan and Somalia.

On November 4, 2020, forces loyal to the TPLF unexpectedly attacked the Northern Command of the Ethiopian Federal Defense Forces. It was believed that the attack was carried out with the intention of taking over the Command and then overthrowing the central government. After several weeks of fighting, the TPLF was defeated. Many lost their lives and limbs, and millions of people in Tigray are in desperate need of help, but the feared civil war thankfully did not materialize. This short but disastrous war has once again scarred and divided this poor nation. But we live in hope.

HOPE FOR ETHIOPIA

There are some who treat hope as wishful thinking, mere desire, fundamentally irrational, an attitude accompanied by fear, the result of false belief, a cause of superstition, poor understanding of a situation, an expression of misguided relationship to the world, etc. But hope is something that enables human beings to devise mechanisms in order to manage events and arrange outcomes. Hope sustains human agency in the face of widespread evil. Indeed, hope is directed toward a good that lies in the future and motivates human beings to devote their energy. However, hope can only be a useful virtue if it goes hand in hand with love.

As Apostle Paul says: "Love is patient and kind; love does not envy or boast; it is not arrogant or rude. It does not insist on its own way; it is not irritable or resentful; it does not rejoice at wrongdoing but rejoices with the truth. Love bears all things, believes all things, hopes all things, endures all things. Love never ends" (1 Cor. 13:4-8 ESV). Based on this, the Danish philosopher Soren Kierkegaard noted: "without love, no hope for oneself; with love, hope for others." So, the value of hope is dependent on its relation to love, for love persists whether hope is disappointed or realized.

Ethiopians ought to hope in love. They also ought to hope towards a good that lies in the future and motivates them to devote their energy. In so doing, they ought to reconsider their ways of thinking and doing things, their outlooks and guiding principles and their cultural values and political relationships. In what follows, I wish to argue that Ethiopia's hope lies in reconditioned social capital, renewed perspective on religion, reformed stance on gender, revolutionized education, restored relationships and transformed lives, revitalized moral agents, reconsidered identity and redesigned statecraft.

RECONDITIONED SOCIAL CAPITAL

Culturally, Ethiopia cannot be understood apart from communitarian culture. This is what defines Africa as a whole. Kenyan-born religious philosopher John Mbiti said, "I am because WE are and, since we are, therefore I am." This dictum seeks to contradict Rene Descartes' well-known pronouncement "I think, therefore I am" and, in so doing, to show the role of others in the self, which, for Descartes, is individualistic and self-sufficient. Mbiti's aphorism is based on the African *Ubuntu* philosophy, which is based on a Zulu phrase, "*Umuntu ngumuntu ngabantu*", which means "A person is a person through other persons." It is not my intention here to discuss issues relating to *Ubuntu* or Mbiti's philosophy in comparison with the individualistic Cartesian assumption. My intention here is to say that *Ubuntu* encourages community, interconnectedness, working together, generosity and hospitality.

Communitarian systems, led by chief-elders, are social networks characterized by reciprocal relationships. Some regard these systems as authoritarian, or even tyrannical, and obstacles to the development of individual consciousness and autonomy. Others might see them as systems that are void of altruism. However, we cannot deny that living in a society, which functions within the framework of trust and trustworthiness and is rich in small and big favors and helpfulness, is a good thing for members of any community.

The term "social capital" is relevant here. This term was not known in Ethiopia until relatively recently. The term is to do with the networks of relationships among people and communities who live in a particular society. These networks of relationships enable people to function properly and effectively. So, it is relevant to the Ethiopian situation. Robert Putnam, in his book *Bowling Alone*, has shown that Lyda Hanifan was the one who first used this term and defined it as "tangible assets" people need in their daily lives. These assets are goodwill, fellowship, sympathy and social intercourse among the individuals and families who make up a social unit. In the Ethiopian context, this social unit includes blood ties within families, clans and tribes as well as marital ties between individuals from different clans and covenantal ties between rival ethnic groups. Ethiopia is a country in which social capital has played a central role across communities at family, clan, larger fraternity, ethnic group and national levels.

Of course, one should not generalize the ways in which social capital functions among different people groups, which have different systems. Some of the systems are still functional while others are redundant. For example, the Amhara social system is different from that of the Oromo, Gurage, Sidama, Hadiya or others. Indeed, as Donald Levine has rightly pointed out, kinship has played a relatively small role in the Amhara social system[1] as compared with other systems. In the pre-Communist Amhara social system, for example, descendants of local dynasties, individuals with successful military track records and clergy in the Orthodox Church enjoyed huge influence within communities. Since the mid-1970s, the social system has mainly been organized under an ecclesiastical hierarchical structure, wherein the authority of the clergy is increasingly paramount.

Among the Oromos, the *Gada* socio-political system has several structures with related positions such as *qallu* (religious or ritual leader of a group), *abba gada* (senior figure elected for an eight year period), *abba dula* (military leader) and *abba bokku* (senior ritual or religious leader within the Gada structure). Other ethnic groups have social structures that are different from the *Gada* system of the Oromos but whose social organization stretches out from extended family to major lineage of several generations categorized by a clan, a set of clans and ethnic clusters.

These structures organize themselves under chief-elders, who are trusted and inspire confidence and respect among the community. They oversee informal associations within the community and protect shared values. They also ensure that family or clan memories are maintained and passed on, conflicts are resolved, funeral and wedding rites are properly carried out, and communities in different villages have consistent and constructive social interactions and harmonious relationships. These social structures have continued to exist even in areas that have experienced religious transition from, for example, paganism to Christianity or Islam. They often make positive contributions to political and legal edifices as well. As community elders seek to pursue reconciliation and restorative justice rather than antagonism and retributive justice, the possibility of societal healing and harmony is much greater.

Such societal structures function within the framework of not only family or clan ties or other interpersonal relationships and shared values. They mainly depend on trust and trustworthiness, which are anchored on the principle and practice of reciprocity at different levels and on which the strength or weakness of the social networks depends. Family and clan members, neighbors and villagers have confidence in one another. They generally expect that other community members will help them in their hour of need. Relationships generally depend on the principle of reciprocity. Those who receive help are expected to reciprocate. For example, gifts are given in kind or cash during illness, weddings, funerals, circumcision events, thanksgiving programs, house-warming parties, business opening events, etc. Strange though it may sound to some cultures, the givers expect the recipients to return their gift, at least, in a matching manner. Gift relations in these communities are characterized by the polar opposites of choice and obligation. But at the heart of all this is trust and trustworthiness.

Since the mid-1970s, these social structures have gradually been undermined, as the country endured 17 years of Marxism-Leninism under the military-turned-civilian government and almost three decades of ethnic-based political ideology promoted by the EPRDF. The former promoted a tyrannical system, where there was only one winner, while the latter inculcated an adversarial and divisive ideology. Under both systems, trust, which is a valuable commodity, was not fairly distributed. The practice of trusting those people from the same family or ethnic background and distrusting all others or even viewing them as enemies became part of the socio-political culture. Under the EPRDF, politics were characterized by bitter rivalry among members even within the same party, where one's survival in a given political position was dependent on the destruction of the other.

The EPRDF politically instrumentalized individuals and communities by applying the Machiavellian principles of "the end justifies the means" and divide-and-rule. As Machiavelli in his *The Prince* describes, the supreme guardians of revolutionary democracy used laws and force, which belonged to both humans and animals respectively. For example, the EPRDF had a policy and practice of what it called periodic evaluations. During evaluations, an organized group would make bogus and unsubstantiated claims against a person or a group. Political action such as demotion or total removal from office would be taken against the accused without any further investigation. These evaluations encouraged politicians to engage in mutual destruction for personal and political gain.

Politicians were led to believe that confusing human minds with cunning schemes, rather than honesty and integrity, would enable them to achieve great things. Indeed, pursuant to Machiavellianism, many accepted that to act contrary to trust, charity, humanity and honesty was acceptable so long as it enabled them to hold onto power. Kinship and patronage played a part in this power game. But it was a game that led to brother turning against brother to overcome each other. Social capital, based on trust and trustworthiness, was undermined.

Mistrust and instability reigned in the country. All of this was exploited by the political masters and enabled them to achieve their political goals unhindered.

For many, political obedience (whether voluntarily or under duress) to the top leadership brought not only victory but also wealth and prosperity. But such an approach developed hostilities and resentments within communities. Family members of other or no ideological persuasions regarded their blood relatives, who were members of the ruling party, as traitors of their own kinsmen and enemies of the common good in favor of what many saw as a divisive, unjust and repressive system. Families within the same clan were divided. Community and religious leaders were believed to be compromised in one way or another and, as a result, lost credibility.

The cumulative result of all this was that social capital was greatly undermined and societal stability threatened. Commitment to restore networks of relationships that center on trust and trustworthiness and are anchored on shared values and healthy reciprocal relationships, has now become indispensable for the future of the Ethiopian nation and her inhabitants. For it is in the context of restored social and relational capital alone that any societal, political and cultural values would have any meaning.

As the late Lamin Sanneh consistently emphasized, attempts to restore social networks of relationships must include the following considerations. First, political mobilization can undermine societal values if it politicizes ethnicity and religion. It remains true that ethnic identity, as well as religious affiliation, cut across national and political boundaries. Still, the politicization of ethnicity and religion can only complicate and damage the relationships and the structures of trust. This means that political office holders should not manipulate religion and ethnicity to their own advantage. Ethnic identity is grounded in loyalty to the ethnic group but it also has divine origin. Religious responsibility is grounded in loyalty to God. So in a sense, there are two competing sovereignties: divine sovereignty, which has a claim on human faith, loyalties, and allegiances, and political sovereignty, which is the nation state and its jurisdiction.

Second, in the Ethiopian context, it is essential to relate the role of social capital to the role of civil society. While the former centers on ethnic loyalties and clan relationships, the latter centers on the voluntary association and organization of life. But both are supposed to be free from political domination and government control. As Sanneh rightly argues, "government is not equipped to deal with issues of solidarity, of mutual trust, of compassion, of caring for one another, of honesty, of integrity, and the virtues of helping others and thinking well of others. These are values and virtues that belong firmly in the domain of civil society."[2] They are also values that belong within the pluralism of languages and ethnic groups in Africa as a whole. As Sanneh would agree, ethnic and linguistic diversity is not an obstacle that we should try to overcome, but rather it is an asset that we should harness. Nation-building can happen only if people are confident in who they are and are not ashamed of their language or the religion they profess.

Third, while celebrating Ethiopia's ethnic and linguistic plurality and seeking to restore social capital and focus on civil society as a necessary vehicle for societal flourishing, we need to be mindful of the importance of the individual. For Ethiopians and indeed Africans as a whole, the notion of *Ubuntu*, where "a person is a person through other persons," remains essential. This corporate consciousness is no longer dismissed as 'primitive,' but it needs to be balanced with individual consciousness, which is different from self-centered individualism. Community or civil society is the domain of life where children grow up as individuals. It is where they are trained in their families' customs and acquire their sense of who they are as human beings and their links with the rest of humanity. That is where their moral development takes place. A society is good only when individuals are good. So, endeavors towards restored social capital must account for the role of the individual within society.

RENEWED PERSPECTIVE ON RELIGION

Hope for Ethiopia also lies in a restored perspective on religion. In addition to traditional religious beliefs and practices, the three major religions of the world form the religious identity of Ethiopia. So, Ethiopia cannot be understood apart from understanding the kind of interactions that have historically existed among Judaism, Christianity and Islam. I refer to Judaism here mainly because I wish to point out the place of the Falasha (emigrant) in Ethiopian history and briefly describe the interactions of Falasha Judaism with Christianity and Islam.

JUDAISM AND CHRISTIANITY

Judaism forms the religious identity of Ethiopia not only through the Judaic elements in Ethiopian Orthodox Tewahido Christianity, but also because of the existence of the Falasha (currently called Beta Israel) in Ethiopia for centuries. There have been four theories concerning the origin of the Falasha.

Some think that they were descendants of Israelites who came with Menelik I, a son of the Queen of Sheba and King Solomon. If this story is valid, then the Falasha have existed in Ethiopia for more than two millennia. But others argue that the Falasha were Jews of the Elephantine on the Nile in Egypt. If that were the case, they must have lived in Ethiopia for centuries as well. Another view is that the Falasha could have been Ethiopian traders who went to South Arabia (now Yemen), converted to Judaism and continued to practice it. But others argue that they were South Arabians who practiced a form of Judaism and had emigrated to Ethiopia.

We simply don't know the origin of the Falasha with any level of certainty. What we are certain about is that the Falasha existed in Ethiopia for centuries; they had their own territory north of Lake Tana. They were numerous in number, part of the social fabric of the nation and were subjects to Ethiopian emperors while maintaining administrative autonomy. They practiced non-Talmudic Judaism faithfully.

Some argue that soon after the introduction of Christianity in Ethiopia in the 4th century, the Falasha were persecuted. We don't know the full story behind persecution in the early periods, but we know that between the 14th and 16th centuries, attempts were made to exterminate the Falasha. It is said that this was due to their collaboration with Ahmed bin Ibrahim El Ghazi (Ahmed the Left-Handed) during his jihadist campaign against the Christian kingdom in the early 16th century AD. But the 17th century saw the death of many Falasha due to fighting with the Christian emperor and refusal to accept forced baptism and conversion to the Christian faith.

Much of the violence was probably politically motivated. But religion was at the heart of the conflict. Indeed, in my view, the battle was raging between two socio-political systems, one that was shaped and guided by Judaism and another by Christianity with the Christian emperor actively on its side. The result was that the Falasha suffered social and cultural prejudices and remained marginalized for centuries until tens of thousands of them were airlifted to Israel between 1980 and 1992 under Israel's policy of repatriation of Jews from across the world.

The Ethiopian state had a socio-political system fused with a Christian religious system. Christianity served as an engine and guide to politics. In its interaction with Falasha Judaism, it served as a force for ill rather than good, violence rather than peace. This should not burden us with guilt, but rather it should enable us to learn from the past so that we are not condemned to repeat the same mistake. This brings me to the interaction between Christianity and Islam.

CHRISTIANITY AND ISLAM

Fifty years ago, J.S. Trimingham asserted that the Christian state of Ethiopia is a "beleaguered fortress in the midst of the sea of Islam."[3] While some accept this assertion, others have challenged it or even sought to speak about the "beleaguered Muslim fortresses" whereby historical relations between the medieval Christian kingdom in the north and Muslim Sultanates in the South East were ones of aggressive expansion by Christian kings.[4] How one understands Ethiopia's history of state formation and its religious journey determines one's position in relation to these opposing views and indeed one's perspective on the impact of Islam on Christianity in Ethiopia. I would argue that while the history of Christianity and Islam in Ethiopia is characterized by the juxtaposition between *positive interactions and periodic conflicts*, the relations between Islam and Christianity in Ethiopia should be assessed on the basis of internal socio-political dynamics and the roles external forces have played on the manner of those interactions and conflicts.

Our assessment must start with the famous encounter in the 7th century (614 AD to be precise) between followers of Mohammed from Mecca and the Axumite kingdom in the north of Ethiopia, where Christianity had already been in existence for three centuries. The story, in brief, is that an Ethiopian king, called the Negus or, as Muslims would call him, Nejashi (614-631), gave shelter to early Muslims from Mecca, who were seeking refuge from persecution. This journey has become a formative event in Islamic attitudes towards Ethiopia. There are at least three views linked to this story. The general view is that the whole event was characterized by royal benevolence, hospitality and, as a result, lasting friendship. Against this, it has been argued that the Axumite Ethiopians were hostile to the pioneers of Islam and ever since have joined hands with the infidels to destroy Islam.[5] The third view is that the Ethiopian king converted to Islam following Mohammed's written invitation and ultimatum and, therefore, Ethiopia was part of *dar al Islam* (land of Islam) and must, therefore, be reclaimed as such.[6]

It is widely accepted that Mohammed wrote a letter, to which the king purportedly showed reverence. In the letter, Mohammed invited the king to follow God and him as the Messenger of God. Some sources claim that he did not give him the ultimatum,[7] while others claim that he did. [8] In later Muslim historiography, it is claimed that the king of Axum had converted to Islam, although he concealed his devotion to

Islam for fear of clergy and the populace.[9] Ethiopian Orthodox Christian scholars accept the story of the king's act of kindness and hospitality to the Meccan refugees but vigorously reject the story of the king's conversion. One argument that supports this view is Mohammed's ordering of Muslims in the Hadith (the collection of his sayings outside the Quran) to "leave the Abyssinians alone as long as they leave you alone." No certainty is possible about all these claims and counterclaims, but radical Islamic elements within and outside Ethiopia have continued to assert that Ethiopia used to be part of the "land of Islam."

Nowadays, outside forces seek to clandestinely cement these claims. The notable example is Turkey, which, like the Ottomans particularly in the 16th and 17th centuries,[10] has developed an interest in the Horn of Africa in general and in Ethiopia in particular. President Erdogan, a few years ago, received an honorary doctorate from the University of Addis Ababa and commissioned the restoration of an ancient mosque and a tomb purported to be that of the Negus, King Nejashi. Having successfully carried out the restoration project to the tomb and the mosque by adopting the Ottoman architectural style, the Turkish government proposed that King Najashi's tomb be added as a route of *umrah*, the non-mandatory pilgrimage made by Muslims. There are some who hope that Turkey's proposal, along with other activities, would pave the way for Ethiopia to reclaim her status as a land of Islam and that Ethiopia's historic enmity to Islam would end. Some might also go so far as to say that this would remove once and for all the fear that remains in the Arab psyche about the "lean-legged" man from Ethiopia destroying the Ka'ba (*Hadith* 666). Would the resulting effect be lasting peace or an enabling of Islam to march southward unhindered?

Second, the current involvement of Turkey and other Arab nations in Ethiopian politico-religious life seems to me to be a continuation of what started in the 7th century and facilitated radicals among Muslims in the southeast and Christians in the north to achieve their evil agenda in the name of religion. It is well known that the ascendancy of Islam in the 7th and 8th centuries became a cause for the decline of the politically and economically powerful Christian empire in Axum. This is believed to have started with the destruction of the Ethiopian trading post in a Red Sea port, followed by successive battles between Ethiopian naval forces and the new Islamic state in Arabia.[11] The antagonism had already started between Ethiopia and Arabia, because in 570 AD (when Mohammed was born) an Ethiopian king had attempted to Christianize Mecca by force as well as undermine the Ka'ba as a pagan pilgrimage site by building a church in Sana'a in Yemen.[12] The attempt failed but caused commercial crisis, which led the Persians to intervene militarily and end the Ethiopian rule in Yemen. Later in the 7th century, Muslim armies overran South Arabia, as a result of which Axum's already weakened trade connection through sea and caravan routes was further affected. This also negatively impacted the direct ecclesiastical link with Alexandria.[13] The isolation of Axum was compounded by the fact that Muslims took Dahlak Islands (now Eritrean territory) and destroyed the port of Adulis in the 8th century. This further weakened Axum and facilitated the ascendancy of Islam, as Muslim traders from Arabia were able to move freely on the trade routes in the north and east of Ethiopia and establish commercial settlements.

In spite of the decline of Axum's political, commercial and spiritual vitality and the loss of its direct link with Alexandria,

Christianity continued to take root in the north and expand southwards.[14] By the 13th century, it had reached the central parts of modern Ethiopia. The expansion of Christianity was coupled with a power-shift from the Semitic Axumite royalty to the Cushitic-speaking Agau dynasty in Lalibela in present-day northern Ethiopia and then to the Semitic-speaking Amhara dynasty in the north, which pronounced itself to be Solomonic.[15] While this power-shift was taking place in the north with the resulting ethnic-based tensions that continue to afflict Ethiopia to this day, Islam was expanding, and Islamic principalities in the central and southeastern parts were established.[16] So how did the Christian kings interact with these principalities?

Christian kings sought to extend their power and forced Muslim sultanates, who had organized themselves under tribal lines, to become tributaries to the Christian kingdom. This inevitably created resentment and resistance, which in turn led to conflicts. Some Christian kings sought to defuse these resentments through political and economic integration. They also attempted to use Ethiopian Muslims for diplomatic missions to Muslim Egypt, which was hostile to Christian Ethiopia. [17] Moreover, closer ties with powerful sultans were probably believed to bring about greater peace and integration, so marital arrangements were used as the main vehicle for this. The best example of this is Emperor Zara Yacob's marriage to Eleni, who was a daughter of a powerful Hadiya sultan called Garad Mohammed. Even this did not stop intermittent rebellions by Muslim sultanates.[18]

In any case, the military achievements of the Ethiopian Empire in Muslim territories made it possible for the Ethiopian Church to be stronger and more confident, but the hatred and fear[19] and repressive policies of the empire toward its territories engendered resentment. Empress Eleni, with her experience and geopolitical knowledge, succeeded in persuading Ethiopian emperors and key leaders of the Muslim principalities to adopt the principle of accommodation and develop friendly interactions toward each other. But such a move incensed both Christian and Muslim radicals, who successfully undermined the principle of accommodation in Christian-Muslim relations. Ethiopian forces continued to attack the Muslim territories. Jihadist clerics from the Arabian Peninsula continued to radicalize Muslim forces.[20]

Third, with a new spirit of anti-Ethiopian *jihad* and a generous supply of Islamic holy war flags and tents from Arabia, the southeastern Muslims engaged in a renewed battle with the Ethiopian Empire in the early 16th century. The battle was led by an ambitious Turkish-backed imam called Ahmad ibn Ibrahim al-Ghazi (also known as Ahmad *Gragn*). Muslim "learned men" from Arabia had convinced him that God had called him to "bring peace and Islam to the land of the Habasha."[21] Ahmad *Gragn* defeated Christian forces, reclaimed Muslim territories, overran most of the northern Christian territories, destroyed churches, burned manuscripts and executed priests and monks. The claim that nine out of ten Christians converted to Islam[22] may be an exaggeration, but large numbers of people converted to Islam in fear for their lives and to be exempt from tax. Those who refused to convert to Islam were either killed or treated as *dhimmis* with *jizyah* tax levied on them. But *Gragn* was defeated and killed by the Christian forces, backed by the Portuguese. What we can notice from all this is that Ahmad *Gragn's jihadist* ideals were fueled by the theological conviction of Arabian forces and the economically and religiously motivated territorial ambition of the Ottoman Empire.

Fourth, Ethiopia, with Christianity at its center, survived, but the situation was complicated again by the violent expansion of the Oromos, who greatly benefited from the devastating effect of Ahmad Gragn's *jihadist* campaign. The Oromos embraced Islam. Their successful campaigns, assimilationist policy and practice, and other political and economic factors enabled them to penetrate the Christian highlands. The Christian kings had no choice but to adopt a moderate attitude towards the Oromos and Muslims. That facilitated the growth of the Muslim population exponentially.[23] Even an imperial decree that Christians and Muslims should live in separate quarters did not stop this tide.[24] The Ethiopian emperors in the 19th century came to believe that the growth and revival of Islam was a great danger to Christianity in Ethiopia and an obstacle to the unity of the country. The military campaigns launched by Egypt and Mahdists in Sudan during Emperor Yohannes IV's rule exacerbated this belief and even turned it into paranoia. The emperor attempted to Christianize communities *en masse* through coercive and tactical relationships with powerful Muslim Oromo chiefs.[25] All this, however, had little effect in Christianizing and uniting the country, as many returned to their former faith and the country remained divided.[26]

Fifth, the positive interactions and periodic hostilities between Islam and Christianity continued until the early 20th century. Emperor Iyasu II had a political vision to reconcile Christian and Muslim sectors in Ethiopia. He felt Muslims were persecuted and were not enjoying equal living standards with Christians. He once said to Muslim leaders: "Though we differ in religion and tribe, I would wish all of us to be united through a nationalist sentiment... cooperation with the rest of your Ethiopian brothers will keep your country united and her frontiers secure." [27] It is believed that Emperor Iyasu – whose father was a former Muslim Oromo chief and whose mother a daughter of a Christian king – was a man of conviction. He sought to make Ethiopia a haven of religious tolerance, which led to an unfounded accusation that he had converted to Islam. He was too liberally minded for his time, too friendly with Muslims, and had developed too much mistrust towards European powers in the region. Moreover, he had a powerful cousin in Tefari Mekonnen (later Haile Selassie), who had him deposed from power and eventually killed.[28]

Sixth, when Haile-Selassie I became Emperor of Ethiopia in 1930, following Empress Zewditu's death, he strengthened the existing tradition where the emperor is the defender of the Ethiopian Orthodox *Tewahedo* faith and the one whose soldiers spread the gospel and *pax Ethiopica*. The empire and the Church were dependent on each other. Islam was both religion and state in the Middle East. So was Christianity in Ethiopia. According to the imperial and ecclesiastical ideology, the invisible divine kingdom could only be advanced through a visible human kingdom whose political goal must be the creation of common national identity under common law and common Christian doctrine. Haile Selassie reinforced this ideology, which had previously helped Ethiopia to defeat foreign powers such as Turkey, Egypt and Italy. Such ideology was preserved and promoted not only by the Amharas and Tigreans, whose ethnic identity came to be intertwined with Orthodox Tewahedo Christianity, but also by Christian Oromos and others. As Orthodox Tewahedo Christianity became the foundation of patriotism, nationalism and personal identity, so also defending Christian faith was equated with defending the country. Christian-centric theocratic ideology was not fully embraced by everyone within the country. The geopolitical situation was changing, as the kingdom of Saudi Arabia was founded (1932), Anglo-Egyptian Sudan gained independence (1956) and Somalia was created as a nation (1960). Internally, poverty and socio-political oppression and injustice were increasing. Marxism-Leninism became a favorable ideology of many intellectuals. This ideology was combined with territorial and identitarian questions.

Seventh, the theocratic ideology along with the monarchy was destroyed in 1974 by a Marxist-Leninist regime, which was toppled in 1991 by another Marxist group that sought to address the marginalization of Muslims in Ethiopia within the context of the policy of ethnic federalism. Over the last 30 years, Islam has grown in confidence and in number. Islamic extremism has also grown at the same time, albeit covertly. The biggest threat to the country in general is Wahhabism, which has been funded by the massive oil wealth of Saudi Arabia and its neighbors over the years.[29] Since the early 20th century, Wahhabism has been exported to the Horn of Africa through the provision of support to mosques, Quranic schools, imams and, nowadays, various humanitarian projects. As a result, a centuries-old moderate form of Sufi Islam is endangered not only in Ethiopia, but in the Horn of Africa as a whole. This is particularly poignant in Somalia due to the ascendancy of Al-Shabab. A struggle for influence between Riyadh and Tehran is evident not only in Somalia but also in Eritrea, Somaliland and the semi-autonomous Somali region of Puntland. Indeed, the Saudis and their allies are now exerting huge military and economic influence in the region. The Sunni-Shiite battle in Yemen is facilitating this more than ever.

From the above historical analysis, three brief conclusions can be drawn. First, interactions between Christians and Muslims in Ethiopia are based on the interpretation of history. Positive interpretation leads to peaceful relations, and negative interpretation results in conflicts. Second, Arabia, Egypt and Turkey have centuries-old socio-political and religious interests in Ethiopia for mainly economic and religious reasons. Third, external forces often hijack positive interactions between Christians and Muslims in Ethiopia for their own politico-religious and economic benefits.

CURRENT SITUATION

Currently, in my view, there are two main concerns. First, nowadays, some in Ethiopia, like the emperors in the 19th century, believe that Egypt and Sudan's contribution to the growth and revival of an extremist form of Islam is a great danger to the unity and integrity of Ethiopia. Some would disagree with this view. Admittedly, a caliphate does not exist in Egypt anymore; nor are there organized Mahdists in Sudan. However, until recently, Sudan was ruled under Sharia law, and Egypt has had very strong radical Islamic movements such as the Muslim Brotherhood and Islamic Jihad. Currently, radical Islamists within the Egyptian government, opposition political parties and other groups seem to be capitalizing on the current tension between Egypt and Ethiopia over the Great Ethiopian Renaissance Dam (GERD) and internal political discontent. The main goal of the Egyptian political establishments and religious groups in all this is not only weakening the Ethiopian state and undermining the GERD project but also promoting an extremist religious vision, at the center of which is seeing an Islamic state in Ethiopia.

Second, the increasing assertiveness of Wahhabist Islam fueled by Saudi Arabian wealth is deeply worrying. Before Prime Minister Haile Mariam Desalegn resigned in 2018, the Ethiopian government attempted to combat Wahhabism in Ethiopia through jailing Wahhabist-leaning leaders and stealthily promoting a moderate form of *Al Ahbash* Islam, which is basically a more sophisticated form of Sufi Islam, whose guiding principle is clerical pacifism. However, all these attempts failed. Prime Minister Abiy Ahmed released the jailed Wahhabist-leaning leaders. He created a platform for Muslim factions to resolve their differences, find a common ground, and work together. Moreover, he facilitated for the Ethiopian Supreme Council of Islamic Affairs to gain a legal personality through parliamentary proclamation. That Islam in Ethiopia is treated equally with Christianity, and Muslims are no longer officially portrayed as evil and enemies of righteousness, which used to be the case a century ago, should be seen as a positive development. The prime minister's attempt to treat Christians and Muslims equally and make Ethiopia a haven of religious tolerance is also commendable.

I fear, however, that inter-ethnic tensions and political discontent are enabling internal and external forces to use the prime minister's good intentions to promote their radical vision. Dr. Abiy Ahmed is an Oromo. While he is a Christian, the majority of Oromos are Muslims. As indicated above, the history of the Oromos in connection to the Christian-Muslim relations in Ethiopia is a very complicated one. Following the Oromos' successful military campaigns, their population growth through mass adoption and procreation and their ability to penetrate the Christian highlands, Christian emperors centuries earlier came to accept the importance of the involvement of the Oromos in running Ethiopia's national affairs. However, the Christians' policy of coerced mass conversion and baptism has left fear and bitterness in the psyche of the Muslims, particularly amongst the Oromos.

Of course, Ethiopian Muslims in Oromia (where the Oromo people are from) and other regions have no reason to feel marginalized or persecuted. There is constitutional provision for religious freedom and equality. Many Muslims have assumed political and administrative positions. And yet, there are many within the Oromos who believe that political processes must center on the fusion of ethnic identity with Islam. Believing a true Oromo is a Muslim, radical elements have used this misguided perspective to incite violence against Christians. As a result, since 2015, many Catholic, Orthodox and Protestant churches and institutions in the Oromia region have been destroyed. Hundreds of Christians, including Oromos, have been brutally murdered. It is alleged that these radical elements within Oromia are supported by forces from within and outside Ethiopia.

While the violence in Oromia region seems to be targeting all Christians, the Ethiopian Orthodox Tewahido Church (EOTC) feels that it is the chief target of ethno-religious extremists and has not been adequately protected by the Ethiopian government security forces. It has now resolved to defend its members and institutions within the country through "non-violent" means. Orthodox Christianity would have no intention to restore its former position where it was both the religion and state in Ethiopia. Nor would it seek to restore a theocratic government, which in the past not only defended but also served as a vehicle to spread the Orthodox Christian faith. However, it goes without saying that even after Ethiopia ceased to be a religious state, for the majority of those in the northern and central parts of Ethiopia, Orthodox Christian faith continues to be the foundation of patriotism and personal and communal identity. There are now signs that radicalism among Muslims is inspiring radicalism among Orthodox Christians.

Where does this leave Ethiopia and her people now? I don't think that a theocratic state that exclusively defends the Orthodox Christian faith will return. Nor do I think that the dream of some radical elements to establish a political government that sustains puritanical Islamic doctrine through a strict application of Sharia will come true in Ethiopia. But as ethnocentric politics has been on the ascendancy, ethno-religious forces that fuse ethnic and religious identities with political goals are getting stronger. So, any success of militant elements within the Orthodox Christian faith, Islam and other Christian traditions could lead to religiously-inspired civil war. This would lead to potential disintegration of Ethiopia and the end of any hope of peace, stability and progress in the Horn of Africa. So, it is absolutely imperative that the government and religious institutions exert every possible effort to tackle religious extremism and its causes within Christianity and Islam.

Since religious diversity is a reality in Ethiopia, a platform where Christians and Muslims can work together is imperative. It was partly this that led to the establishment of the Inter-Religious Council of Ethiopia (IRCE), which is made up of the Ethiopian Orthodox Tewahedo Church, the Ethiopian Catholic church, the Ethiopian Evangelical Church Mekane

Yesus, the Ethiopian Kale Heywet Church, the Evangelical Churches Fellowship of Ethiopia, the Ethiopian Seventh-Day Adventist Church and the Supreme Council of Islamic Affairs. The IRCE is not designed as a platform for religious dialogue. Its goal is to promote sustainable peace, development and national unity. Through their involvement in the IRCE, the seven religious institutions and their respective members display their commitment to Ethiopia as a nation-state.

In Christian belief, a universal community is created through Christ. Members of this community see themselves as heavenly and earthly citizens. As earthly citizens, the majority of Christians in Ethiopia understand belonging to a nation state as relevant. In Islamic belief, a universal community called *umma*, unitary reality of universal brotherhood, is created. Belonging to *umma* is belonging to a reality for which nationality is irrelevant. It is my understanding, however, that despite their commitment to *umma*, the majority of Ethiopian Muslims see Ethiopia as their home. The leadership of the Supreme Council of Islamic Affairs does not demand Islam to be both religion and state. The majority of Ethiopian Muslims are not spectators but participants in politics, business, media, diplomacy and education, which shows that nationality is relevant for them. This is not to deny the existence of some radical Muslims who have differing views and ideals.

For radical Muslims, religion and politics are intertwined in Islam. Lamin Sanneh has argued that a more careful reading of the sources of Islamic thought will indicate that Islam is also profoundly aware of the importance of religion as an institution of civil society. The Quran speaks of the Caliphate only in moral terms relating to trust, stewardship, and creation care. On this basis, Sanneh argues that religion in Islam is not a political edict or an ordinance of government because faith is an attribute of the moral conscience. Sanneh acknowledges that the fact that Islam is not a pacifist religion (although there have been pacifist Muslim voices) makes Christian-Muslim engagement difficult. However, in the Ethiopian context, real engagement in dialogue with Islam might help advance the prospect of a refashioned national socio-political order inspired by a sense of the holy and the transcendent, and grounded in common creation and the unity of the human family, and united by moral ties of rights and duties.

This is consistent with the Ethiopian Constitution, which in Article 3:2 provides for "nations, nationalities and peoples as well as all religious communities of Ethiopia to live together in equality and unity." As a result, Muslims and Animists are treated as equal citizens with Christians, and Protestant evangelical Christians are treated as equal citizens with Orthodox and Catholic Christians.

As Sanneh argues, the principle of equality before the law presumes that we came into this world on equal terms and will leave it on equal terms. That fact is in line with our equal standing as created in the image and resemblance of God, the Ruler of the universe. This means that no one – whether Christian, Muslim, or Animist – stands above the law, and no one is beneath the law in the sense of being undeserving of the protection and safeguard of the law. Political "rulers are stewards of that teaching and are liable to moral accountability for it. Political stewardship here creates an overlap with the domain of the moral conscience."[30]

This notion of equality is further augmented in Article 11, which provides for the separation of state and religion, and prohibits the state from interfering in the affairs of religion and vice and versa. This article was interpreted during the EPRDF era as saying that the state had nothing to do with religion and vice versa. In the new political order, it was thought that interethnic harmony, national unity, and societal flourishing could be attained without the need for religion. It was a form of secularist humanism. This amounted to a denial of the fact that Ethiopia's societal and cultural values are shaped by religion. This also seemed to force members of religious institutions to maintain divided loyalty to a nation state as earthly citizens and a religious community as heavenly citizens. Such Marxist-driven constitutional interpretation (or misinterpretation) is now being corrected.

To be sure, the modern Ethiopian state cannot afford to be a religious state. Nor can it be rendered a purely secular state, in which religious freedom is enjoyed but without religion playing any role in public life. However, while it is true that interchanging politics with religion or vice versa can potentially lead to sacred truth and secular agency becoming indistinguishable, in the Ethiopian context, the role of religion in public life is not optional. The question as to how this can be managed is not yet answered, however.

Sanneh has argued that the American perspective on separation of church and state may offer a useful example to articulate the distinction between the sacred and secular. In the American case, the religious has ceded ground in the secular sphere, but it has not been stripped of public interest entirely. This might indeed provide an example, but Ethiopia will need to develop a contextually relevant formula, which maintains the separation of state and religion but accounts for the fact that 97% of the population are adherents of Christianity and Islam. One might rightly ask whether religion can maintain its freedom and independence while playing some role in the public square. This will be discussed later in the book. Here, let me introduce Article 27 of the Ethiopian Constitution.

This article provides for the freedom of religion, which includes *any Ethiopian* adopting a belief of her or his choice and manifesting that belief through "worship, observance, practice, teaching or expressing." That individual has freedom to become a member of an organized religious body, which has freedom to propagate its religious convictions through preaching and establishing educational institutions. Article 27 further protects individuals and communities from becoming subject to religious coercion or restriction. It has provision for parents to guide their children according to moral principles and values based on their religion. It also puts limits to religious freedom in that religious freedom must not endanger the fundamental rights and freedoms of others such as public safety, peace, health, education and public morality.

Finally, according to Article 90, education shall be provided in a manner that is free from "religion, political partisanship, and cultural influence." This article has been interpreted as saying that no religious and theological education should be taught in secondary schools and higher educational institutions. Nor should theological institutions be recognized or accredited by the Ministry of Education or a relevant government body. In my view, this is an ideologically driven interpretation. The article should be interpreted as saying that education shall be provided in a manner that is free from religious dogma or any proselytizing intentions. This applies to Marxist socialism or neo-liberalism, African communitarianism or Cartesian individualism. In any case, for as long as the current federal constitution exists and any future amendment maintains these four constitutional provisions, it will be possible for all religions in Ethiopia to have a level playing field.

Religious freedom and equality of religions in Ethiopia can have societal benefits. Emperor Iyasu II embraced this attitude in the early 20th century. Iyasu's father was a former Muslim Oromo chief, while his mother was a daughter of the famous Christian Emperor, Menelik II. Iyasu wanted Christians and Muslims 'to be united through a nationalist sentiment' and cooperate with each other to keep their country 'united and her frontiers secure.' [31] Emperor Iyasu sought to make Ethiopia a haven of religious tolerance. In agreement with this vision, I would argue that the societal benefits that result from religious freedom and equality of religions in Ethiopia could only be reaped in the context of tolerance.

Tolerance as one's ability to stomach the existence of differing opinions or behaviors, or beliefs they might dislike or disagree with, is a difficult concept for many Ethiopian Muslims and traditional Christians to accept. This is obviously different in western societies, which are influenced by social and political liberal philosophy and in which tolerance has become the cardinal virtue of all behaviors concerning religion, race, sexual orientation, political persuasion, etc. This philosophy has nurtured secular humanism. In this context, those who violate the principle of tolerance are labeled as intolerant and unfit to participate in a polite society. In Ethiopia, on the other hand, political and religious intolerance has persisted. Despite this, however, Christianity and Islam have co-existed for over a millennium. While secular humanism does not fit the societal fabric of Ethiopia, it will take time for tolerance and democratic pluralism to take root in Ethiopia.

The accusation against Islam is that it lacks tolerance and

expressions of democratic pluralism. Lamin Sanneh, however, contends that Islam is "endowed with the capacity for tolerance and democratic pluralism."[32] Obviously, not all Muslims would embrace this claim. Sanneh himself admits that "tolerance and pluralism are not extrinsic to Islamic religious culture."[33] This is because the principles of jihad in Islam are not consistent with tolerance and democratic pluralism. As Sanneh puts it: "Jihad shares the secular view that tolerance is not compatible with religion. When tolerance excludes religion, it leaves only two contestants holding the field: the champions of tolerance who oppose religion and the jihadists who are at war with tolerance."[34] France, a fiercely secular state, is a modern example of this untenable situation. In his much-criticized book, *Who is Charlie*,[35] Emmanuel Todd argued that France's real threat is not Islam but a "new religion of radical secularism." Whether or not this is a biased view against anti-political Islam forces, his book reveals how jihadists and secularists are at each other's throats in France.

Jihad and radical secularism are not desirable for Ethiopia. Accordingly, Muslims and Christians alike must reject Jihad and radical secularism in Ethiopia and engage with one another. In this scenario, they can champion the cause of peace and justice not only in Ethiopia but also in the Horn of Africa as a whole. Historically, Christians and Muslims have coexisted in Ethiopia for 1,416 years. They have managed their coexistence by combining social capital with religious principles. There have been moments in history when their relationship faced challenges, but both Christians and Muslims in Ethiopia understand that peaceful coexistence is not optional but necessary. To strengthen this culture of coexistence and pass it on to the next generation, Christians and Muslims must realize that peace is more than an absence of conflict. Peace is an unshak-able value and culture founded on trust, understanding, mutual respect, and love within communities. So inter-religious coop-eration to achieve peace and justice is vital. It also lays a foun-dation for inter-faith dialogue.

REFORMED STANCE ON GENDER

Ethiopia has many cultural norms. One cultural norm, which I think defines all other customs and practices, is *patriarchy*. Ethiopian society is male-dominated, so fathers and sons are treated as more important than mothers and daughters. This raises the question of gender identity, which is part of what it means to be human. In Ethiopia, by and large, the difference between male and female human beings is understood only on the basis of biological difference. This is partly based on the ancient way of life, where women married early, had children and stayed at home, while men went to farm, hunt and fight. This led to women being treated as inferior physiologically, and in experience, age and intelligence. As a result, the superiority of fathers and sons and the inferiority of mothers and daugh-ters became a cultural norm.

In the Ethiopian Constitution, Article 35, however, provides that women have equal rights with men in societal life in general and marriage in particular. Taking the historical legacy of inequality and discrimination, the Constitution also provides that women are entitled to "affirmative measures" to enable them to gain education and actively engage in political and economic activities. The Constitution also prohibits laws, customs, and practices that are harmful to women. In addition to this, the Constitution has clauses, which specify women's rights to maternal health and employment. While much progress has been made in the country in terms of gender equality and complementarity, the culture of patriarchy prevails.

Patriarchal culture, I would argue, hinders human development and relational restoration in Ethiopia. This is acknowledged the world over. The fifth of the 17 initiatives in the Sustainable Development Goal (SDG) agenda is: "achieve gender equality and empower all women and girls." Many nations across the world, including Ethiopia, have signed up to this goal to be achieved by 2030. The goal, in this agenda, is not to enable women and girls to exercise power over men or each other. Rather, it is to enable women and girls to overcome socio-cultural challenges and bring out their intellectual and creative potential so that they can make their way in this world with courage and competence and contribute fully to societal flourishing. This idea stands contrary to the influential cultural belief of our patriarchal society where women and girls are seen as inferior secondary beings in socio-political and religious spheres.

For the Orthodox, Catholics and Protestant evangelicals, the conception of God as the creator and sustainer of life is at the heart of their anthropology. The majority of Ethiopians also believe that at the center of the means God has furnished for the flourishing of the human family are mothers and girls as life givers. Full recognition of this should include an unequivocal belief in equality between women and men and mechanisms through which this belief is put into practice. This, however, has not been the case so far.

The issue is often clouded by the debate over two related but different ideas. Some would argue that women are seen as equal with men in fundamental worth and social status, hence deserving the same rights and opportunities as men. Others would argue that women and men have different but complementary roles in marriage, family life and leadership. The former view technically is called egalitarianism, while the latter is called complementarianism. But the notion of gender complementarity is only valid within the context of gender equality, without equivocation. This means that old stereotypes, which portray women as inferior beings even in nature, must be questioned and challenged. This includes portrayals of women in the ancient world, where, for example, Greek and Jewish philosophers and Christian theologians viewed women as inferior and evil. Ethiopia's hope lies in producing a generation of women and men with a corrected perspective on humanity and human worth, particularly on the ways in which women are viewed and treated. This starts with accepting that Ethiopian society is still heavily centered around men, and life for women continues to be extremely tough.

I grew up observing how tough life was for women in a remote part of southern Ethiopia. I was the oldest of nine children. I had my mother, six sisters and my aunts around me. I was the first born and a male. My two brothers arrived after my six sisters. This gave me a higher position next to my father within the family. I received the best treatment in every way and did very little even for myself, as my sisters did things for me like washing my feet at night. But my mother carried the heaviest burden. Giving birth to a child every two years for 20 years was difficult enough. She also milked the cows, fetched water from the river on her back, collected firewood, cleaned the house (including the cattle barn), ground the grain and cooked for multitudes. The daily routines were punishing. She would wake up before everyone else and go to bed after everyone else every day and night. She had no break except when she was in her maternal chamber after giving birth to a child. When they grew up, my sisters helped her. I helped with farming and looking after the livestock, but I was regarded as superior to and more important than my female family members. There was gender inequality in my parents' home, which is not, of course, the case in my own home. It is my strong conviction that Ethiopia's socio-political and economic problems cannot be tackled without tackling gender inequality and its consequences.

Some of the manifestations of these consequences are socio-cultural practices such as Female Genital Mutilation (FGM), early marriage and modern slavery. In Ethiopia, FGM practices are so deeply entrenched in societal systems that even mothers, who as young girls endured this horrendous and traumatic experience, have their daughters mutilated. All of my six sisters suffered FGM. Millions of girls in Ethiopia experience genital mutilation to this day. To this is added another modern phenomenon, where young girls are removed from schools either to be sent to a foreign country as brides for wealthier men they have never met or to be sent to a Gulf country as maids to become their family's source of income. Some husbands also send their young wives, even after they have had children. Many experience unimaginable physical and psychological hardships. Many end up in jail for one reason or another and face even more suffering. Among those who return, some are mentally unstable, and many are advanced in age. For those who are unmarried and advanced in age, pursuing education and finding a suitable husband become extremely difficult. When attempts to start a new life through pursuit of business ventures and marital arrangements are unsuccessful, many return to the Gulf again to go through the same suffering.

It is difficult to see how young girls can resist this in the face of increasing pressure from their families and peers, economic difficulties in the countryside and rising unemployment among university and college graduates, etc. There are encouraging attempts in the political sphere – with assistance from some non-governmental organizations – to establish legal mechanisms to protect women, to increase educational opportunities for girls, to expand economic opportunities for women, to promote the health and safety of women and girls, and to encourage women to participate in socio-political activities.

While individuals and governmental and non-governmental organizations may exert every possible effort to stop socio-cultural practices that are believed to be harmful to women, it is women themselves who can bring about lasting solutions to the problems they face. Efforts should be centered on raising women's critical consciousness regarding social and political conditions, which are characterized by inequalities of treatment and opportunity. This effort would provide them with a deeper understanding of the socio-economic, cultural and political forces that shape their lives.

Alternative views can be suggested, but hope for Ethiopia lies in people of influence in political and religious spheres within the country and agencies and nations across the world joining hands to address societal ills that center on and result from gender inequality. Central to these efforts, as argued above, should be an awareness program. But hope for Ethiopia also lies in people of influence in political spheres taking practical action.

Dr. Abiy Ahmed's government has brought some reforms in

the area of gender such as appointing women to 50% of cabinet positions and as heads of the Supreme Court and the Electoral Board. But what is happening at the federal level is not happening at the regional, zonal and district levels. Nor is much happening in church contexts, although some churches are trying to address gender issues.

Christians know that social problems were not intended by God but instituted by society and culture. So, they must advocate against gender-related problems through a method that combines anthropological and socio-cultural issues with biblical frameworks. They must do that with confidence and with Jesus as their prime example. Jesus viewed women as those with qualities of service, trust, diligence, perseverance, sacrifice, commitment and love. He departed from the prevailing norm in the ways in which he interacted with and treated women. For Jesus, women were not second-class citizens but persons of intrinsic value equal to that of men. I would also argue that there is no compelling evidence that Paul viewed women as inferior to men. For Paul, Jesus set the ultimate example for us that relationships between women and men should be characterized by self-giving love and sacrificial service rather than a desire to control, compete and engage in conflict. Christians are called to be models of restored relationships in order to address the deeply entrenched cultural norms where women are treated as inferior to men.

REVOLUTIONIZED EDUCATION

So far, I have argued that Ethiopia's hope lies in a reformed stance on gender, renewed perspective on religion and reconditioned social capital. None of this would succeed without education, so the ways in which education is designed and delivered is absolutely vital. There is a general belief in Ethiopia that education is key to societal progress, but the country's educational journey has been extremely bumpy.

HISTORICAL BACKGROUND

Historically, education in Ethiopia started with a traditional church school system. This has been practiced particularly in the Ethiopian Orthodox Church. The church school system involves learning the ancient language Ge'ez and its literature, religious music and poetry, the Old and New Testaments, the history of Ethiopia, rules and disciplines, the Ethiopian calendar and various arts and crafts including calligraphy and manuscript making. The whole process is estimated to take 20 to 30 years, and the objective is to repeat the information from memory rather than process and critically analyze the information. The same is true for Muslims. Students in Madrasas pursue rote learning, which mainly focuses on memorizing the Quran. Repetition of existing information enables religious students to acquire foundational knowledge about religion, literature and history. Such a method also equips the students to jealously, albeit uncritically, safeguard their respective traditions. But it does not enable them to gain deeper understanding of memorized information, learn new knowledge, develop analytical competence and deal with new and complex concepts.

This is not to suggest, however, that the intellectual tradition was limited to mere memorization, as there were some who engaged in rational and critical reasoning; people who dared to think unconventionally and from a new perspective.

The Ewstatewosites (followers of Ewstatewos in the 14th century) successfully argued against the Egyptian Coptic Church's decree against the practice of the observance of two Sabbaths (Saturday and Sunday). The Estifanosites (followers of Abba Estifanos) critically questioned and then rejected the reverence demanded by the political and religious authorities for icons, crosses and the monarch in the 15th century. The 17th century's philosopher Za'ra Ya'qob's metaphysics, ethics, rational theology and psychology reflected the kind of critical thinking that may have existed at the time, although these sorts of intellectual efforts were very unpopular within the ecclesiastical and political hierarchy. In the 17th century, Christian scholars in Gonder produced a series of commentaries on the Bible known as the *Andemta* commentary tradition. Christological controversies between 17th and 19th centuries are also examples of the kind of vibrant intellectual tradition that existed in Ethiopia until the 19th century. After that, however, the method of learning and the components of the materials taught were tightly controlled by the political and ecclesiastical hierarchies, who resorted to adopt a system of rote and uncritical learning and ensured that diversity of views and critical examination of existing wisdom and practices were not to be tolerated.

Furthermore, no attempts, it seems, were made to introduce the study of science, mathematics, arts, foreign languages and literature. The cumulative effect of all this is that people could not be produced to run statecraft, diplomacy, commerce and industry. Even more so, the country could not experience intellectually underpinned moral, political and economic progress. This was the case until the early 20th century when a government-sponsored "secular" educational system was introduced. But the trend of opening government-sponsored schools was very limited, with only two schools in the whole of the country. The first public school was established in Addis Ababa in 1907, and a year later, a primary school opened in Harer. Those who were lucky enough to attend those schools learnt foreign languages, elementary mathematics and science along with religious subjects. But they were very few. That changed when Catholic and Protestant mission schools were opened in Addis Ababa and different parts of the country. It must be said that it was those mission schools, particularly after the fascist Italian troops left the country in 1941, which provided many of the educated people in Ethiopia.

CRISIS AND SOLUTIONS

Seven decades after the Italians left Ethiopia, there are probably more than 40,000 schools, about 50 universities, and many vocational and industrial colleges. However, the education system has been in crisis. There are at least four chief reasons for the crisis.

The first reason relates to the teaching profession. At the root of this problem is that for decades the majority of teachers in primary and some secondary schools have been recruited from poor-performing backgrounds and received minimal or short-term training. Ethiopia's brightest and best do not want to become teachers, because teaching as a profession is looked down upon and teachers are generally under paid. The result has been a very high turnover in schools. The recent attempt by the government to create a sharp increase in wages and embark on a large-scale skills training program is hoped to improve the situation.

The second key reason is government policy in relation to mother tongue education since the 1990s. Teaching children in the same language spoken at home and within the community during the early years is believed to have pedagogical advantages in terms of better understanding and developing language-learning skills. But mother tongue education in Ethiopia was introduced not mainly on pedagogical grounds but as part of the politicization of education, because it was seen as a human rights issue and political panacea for the discontent relating to ethnic identity. This came with two problems. First, primary school children lacked basic skills of literacy and numeracy in all languages, namely mother tongue (the early age medium of instruction), Amharic (the federal working language) and English (the language of science, technology and international communication). Also, teachers were not properly trained to handle this, as the policy was hastily implemented. The majority of the teachers – poorly trained, underpaid and already ashamed of their profession – became deeply unhappy and resentful. Many harbored often unspoken but deep rejection of the foundations and essence of the policy. The result is that standards and learning outcomes remained very low, and schools were full of almost illiterate and consistently under-performing pupils.

The third key reason for the crisis was that the curriculum was not developed in such a way that students could develop their competence through analytical, critical and reflective thinking as well as through practical and occupational skills. Students did not even learn 50% of the materials they were supposed to cover for their respective grades. The average score in different grades was very low. Less than 50% of those who sat grade 10 national examinations scored the required grades to enter grade 11. Even amongst those who managed to enter grade 11, the majority did not have the expected knowledge, aptitudes and skills.

The fourth reason was that the higher education intake strategy of so-called "70:30" privileged engineering over other sciences. Forty percent of university entrants were made to join engineering programs, 30% natural and other applied sciences and 30% social sciences. The chief reason for such a focus was to advance innovation and technological development. This is to be commended, but such an imbalanced and biased focus probably has done more harm than good. For one thing, many students with a weak base of science and mathematics joined the science and engineering programs, struggled to perform, and after graduating, to sustain their interest in the profession. For another, many of those who joined politics for example did not have the necessary skills in the area of political philosophy and economics. Furthermore, as there are fewer graduates from the field of social sciences, the number of thought leaders in the socio-cultural and political sphere significantly diminished.

Those who manage to complete their education through this educational system struggle to compete for jobs due to their poor command of language as well as the lack of required knowledge, aptitudes and skills. This is exacerbated by the sheer imbalance between graduates and available jobs. It is therefore estimated that more than half a million college and university graduates are unemployed. The resulting effect of all this is that the present system of education fast reproduced a surplus of jobless graduates, who are demanding, angry and easily radicalized and fall prey to extremist ethno-political and religious forces.

WORRYING DEVELOPMENTS

Even more worryingly, education is no longer viewed as the chief means through which societal, familial and individual life can be improved. Leaving school and earning money in the capital Addis Ababa, and other parts of the world such as Sudan, the Middle East, South Africa or Europe (via Libya or Yemen) has become something many dream about. Ethiopia, as a result, is a country of school-leavers. As a government document called 'Ethiopian Education Development Roadmap' shows, in the last 20 years alone an average of 45% of children left school before fifth grade; 60% before eighth grade; 75% before tenth grade; and 93% failed to register in twelfth grade. These figures look incredible, but they probably are true.

This was driven home to me about two years ago when my wife and I employed a house worker. She was from the south. She had left school after starting tenth grade to go to Beirut to work as a housemaid. It was not a successful venture. A year or so later, she returned from Beirut. She did not go back to school mainly due to pressure from her parents to find another job instead. When my wife and I tried to interview her in Amharic, she said she could not speak Amharic. When I asked her in her mother tongue if she could read Amharic, she said she could not. Out of utter disbelief and despair, I wrote down a list of names and asked her to try to read them. After a few agonizing minutes and with a lot of clues and prompting, she managed my name. There are millions throughout Ethiopia whose future is darkened or even destroyed like that of our bright and beautiful house worker. Hope for Ethiopia lies in reversing this kind of crisis in the long term.

While overemphasis on the pedagogical advantages of

mother tongue education and using it as a means to address political injustices should be corrected, the usefulness of early years mother tongue education must be accepted. Along this line, the proposals in the Roadmap that mother tongue as a medium of teaching and learning should be reduced to children of 4-6 years of age, English as a subject should start from first or third grade, and Amharic as a subject should start from first grade are reasonable. To argue otherwise is to continue to use education as a political tool used mainly by those politicians whose children attend the best schools within Ethiopia or abroad. I hope that the new educational system will foster holistic development, promote critical thinking, spur entrepreneurship and innovation, produce competent professionals able to compete in the global arena and build citizens with strong ethical and moral values.

EDUCATION AND RELIGION

One glaring weakness in the Ethiopian educational system is that while it recommends moral teaching to be included in the curriculum, on the whole, it goes along with the Ethiopian government's policy where religion is not part of the curriculum at any level. This is unfortunate because the absence of religious inquiry in the public and intellectual arena means a lack of understanding of the religious and philosophical grounds upon which the nation was founded.

Lamin Sanneh has rightly argued that religion must be part of the school curriculum in Africa. Children must learn what Christianity, Islam, and even traditional religions have to say about the human being in relation to the Creator. They need to grapple with the questions as to who and what God is, what

God requires of human beings or what commandments he has given them, and how those commandments can be fulfilled within the context of family, clan, community, and even the nation. These topics are appropriate for inquiry because while individualism is alien to Africa, religion is innate.

Sanneh understands the importance of individual conscience and the virtue of freedom even in the African context. But freedom is not license to do whatever one pleases, not being accountable to anyone. Indeed, freedom, for Sanneh, is not value-free nor neutral. Freedom means responsibility, otherwise, it becomes damaging to societies as well as to individual character. So, we take care of freedom in a way that uses it to enhance our capacity for moral choice. But without religion included in education, moral progress and societal flourishing cannot be attained in a meaningful and sustainable manner. I would, therefore, argue that it is vital to offer religion at secondary schools and religious studies at universities in Ethiopia. I wish to give four reasons to support this argument.

First, the history and identity of Ethiopia as a nation cannot be understood apart from the Judeo-Christian and Islamic faiths. Understanding the past and present religious literature, music, art, religious ideas, myths and symbols is vital to understanding the diverse socio-cultural and historical foundations and values that constitute Ethiopia as a nation. These foundational values are more important than ever, as identitarian ideology, economic nationalism, and religious extremism are rapidly growing in our world.

Second, Ethiopia is a deeply religious country with 97.3% of the population claiming to have a religious affiliation of some sort. Indeed, for the vast majority of Ethiopians (like in all African countries), the idea that they are believers is center stage. But fervent religious devotion alone is not sufficient for a society to flourish. Faith unexamined can become an instrument of death and destruction rather than peace, unity and development, as is the case in Somalia, Nigeria, Mali, Egypt, Libya, etc. Faith must be thought through in a neutral environment, where it can be critically examined and constructive frameworks can be developed towards societal progress, order and cohesion.

The third reason is that academic inquiry of religion enables Ethiopians to counter two threats. The first threat is posed by the fusion of ethnic and religious identities with political goals. The second threat is posed by religious extremism. These threats often have irrational foundations, which only rational discussions can counter. Academic inquiry of religion can help produce people who can stand on the side of reasoned faith and balanced inter-ethnic and religious interactions.

The fourth and final reason is serious academic studies of religious ideas, and ancient sacred and other writings could create a new generation of Ethiopians who are able to develop religious or theological frameworks and articulate them responsibly and constructively. This could have practical results in terms of inter-religious understanding, shaping public beliefs about God and morality and developing public theology that can help bring faith to bear in the world of politics, contributing to public policies and promoting the common good.

Even in secular states like France, Emmanuel Todd (*Who is Charlie*) admits that in regions where Catholicism plays a central role in societal life, better school results, fewer family problems, lower unemployment and better economic success can be observed. These positive outcomes are most likely due to the Church's teaching against selfishness and mass narcissism, and its anti-individualist morality. The Catholic tradition also promotes family and community as networks of support and mutual aid and provides the necessary layers of protection against market forces. Todd refers to these regions as inegalitarian and rudely labels the Catholicism in these regions and elsewhere in Europe as 'zombie'. This again can be treated as biased and unfair. Pertinent to our discussion here, the kind of social networks of support that exist within these traditional and predominantly Catholic regions even in secular France are similar to the kind of social networks of support in Ethiopia. I earlier referred to these networks as *social capital*, which plays a central role across communities at family, clan, ethnic and even national levels. At the heart of these networks of relationships is religion, whose history and teaching must be properly understood in order for Ethiopian society to flourish and enjoy moral and intellectual progress. This can only be achieved if religion is part of the curriculum at secondary schools and universities.

RESTORED RELATIONSHIPS AND TRANSFORMED LIVES

Human history is never tidy, and Ethiopia is no exception. Employing shrewd diplomacy, political marriages or economic patronage, preaching unity around the myth of "Mother Land" or introduction of political administrative structures along ethnic lines have not healed historic wounds. In my view, Ethiopia's socio-political problems are not the outcome of failure to arrange brilliant political and economic structures. Rather, Ethiopia's problems are the outcome of broken relationships. The poor, the diseased, the hungry, and socially alienated symbolize the brokenness of self and society in Ethiopia. Ethiopia's hope, therefore, lies in restoring these broken relationships, which is more than lifting approximately 30 million people, who live on less than $2 per day, out of poverty.

Restoring relationships, I would argue, is dealing with societal ills that have robbed millions of people of self-worth. It is also healing individuals and communities that have been wounded due to ethnic and religious conflicts, political domination, economic exploitation and cultural imposition. In order for relationships to be restored, differences must be listened to and understood; every individual and community must appreciate that their wound is not unique; and conflicts must be resolved through repentance, forgiveness and reconciliation. Relational restoration in society can then be achieved at local and national levels.

Restored relationships create transformed individuals and communities. Transformed individuals and communities can transform society and the world. This transformation can trickle down to governments, businesses and civil societies. Civil societies, for example, can provide a voice for communities, use social capital to bring communal peace and harmony, engage in humanitarian activities, advocate for policy changes to enable transformation and hold governments to account. Government can bring about transformation through formulating good policies, ensuring public welfare and societal stability, delivering and protecting public goods and through providing education, health and other public services. Businesses can bring about lasting economic change in society by creating wealth and jobs and becoming an economic engine that generates resources, which can be used to lift the poor out of poverty and to provide education and health services. The cumulative effect of all this is societal change. But true societal change is achieved when minds and lives are truly changed.

TRANSFORMED MINDS AND LIVES

There are countless numbers of movements made up of people who want to change Ethiopian society. These movements look like what Bryan Wilson many years ago called the religious "movements of protest" or "revitalization" movements.[36] He categorized these movements as *Conversionist*, *Revolutionist*, *Introversionist*, *Manipulationist*, *Thaumaturgical*, *Reformist*, and *Utopian*. These movements, in Wilson's view, existed among "tribal and third-world peoples." Wilson classified them according to the "religious sect model."

For example, the *Conversionist* claims that God changes individuals in order for them to change a corrupt world. The *Revolutionist* or "Millennial" depends on God to overturn or remove the existing social order, the process of which could involve force, if necessary. The *Introversionist* believes that God has called us to abandon the world in order to enjoy the holiness gained thereby. The *Manipulationist* insists that societal and individual problems can be overcome through acquiring specialist knowledge and techniques. The *Thaumaturgical* claims that God will care for us in this evil world by working miracles, so individuals must be enabled to experience the extraordinary effects of the magical or supernatural in order to escape their problems. The *Reformist* accepts a place in the world and believes that she must use her supernaturally endowed gifts and abilities in order to be "the leaven in the lump" of society and amend the world. The *Utopian* is an idealist or separatist, who believes that God has called humans to reconstruct the world by using their own specification without necessarily seeking divine intervention. These classifications are broadly relevant to the Ethiopian society.[37]

I do not think that those who will be able to address Ethiopia's socio-political, moral and economic problems will be *Revolutionists* with their unconstitutionality and violent activities. Nor will they be *Introversionists* with their world-denying attitude or *Utopians* with their separatist, all-knowing and self-sufficient stance. *Manipulationists* with their claim of specialist knowledge and mind techniques or *Thaumaturges* with their miraculous and magical claims are not going to address Ethiopia's societal ills either.

We need a multitude of *Conversionists* who are open to be changed in order to change Ethiopia, Africa and the world. We also need *Reformists* who are open to use their God-given gifts and abilities in order to mend our broken country and continent. *Conversionists* and *Reformists* are "the wise" through whom societal transformation is achieved. But we cannot expect all 110 million Ethiopians to be *Conversionists* and *Reformists*. That is, we cannot expect every single Ethiopian to use her/his gifts and abilities to heal and mend the country. Nor can we expect every single Ethiopian to be changed in order to change Ethiopia. Transformation requires a critical mass of infectious people and institutions. This critical mass of the "the wise" can only be built through a process of multiplication or reproduction.

How Many?

I would like to illustrate my point here by referring to the spread or reproductive value of coronavirus or COVID-19. Coronavirus is a peculiar type of virus that can cause a highly transmissible disease. For example, if one person is infected by the earliest variant, she or he can potentially infect three other people. This means that if 10 people are infected, they can infect 30 people. This figure grows to 90, 270, etc. and can reach over 400 within a month. Scientists refer to the reproductive value of the virus as R and advise governments to keep the R number under one person. Failure to do so would result in the death of many. In order to multiply a critical mass of transformed people, the R number (metaphorically speaking) should go up rather than down. But like the spread of coronavirus, society is transformed when a reform or change idea spreads from one person to many or when a minority opinion becomes a majority belief. But is it possible to determine the number of change agents whose minority opinion could change existing social convention?

In 2011, scientific research was carried out by the Social Cognitive Networks Academic Research Center at Rensselaer Polytechnic Institute (RPI) in the U.S. The research report was published in the journal *Physical Review E*. Researchers used the P number. According to the study, when the P number increases to the critical value of 10%, -- i.e. 10% of a population is committed to the idea that change agents consistently promote -- the minority opinion will become the prevailing opinion of the entire population.

Other research centers have used different theoretical models and observations and proposed a wide range of possible thresholds for the size of effective critical mass that is capable of changing social conventions. The proposals range from 10% of the population to 40%. In 2018, the University of Pennsylvania and the University of London carried out an online experiment, whose result was published in the journal *Science* (*Vol.*

360, Issue 6393, pp 1116-1119). Their conclusion was that the size of the required critical group for initiating change by over-turning the established behavior is 25% of the population.

Given the wide range of views, I do not wish to go along with either the 10% or the 25% figure. I wish to take the average, which is 17.5% (18%). This obviously is an approximate figure, but if we take this as a benchmark, we need 18 million transformed Ethiopians in order for Ethiopia to become a socially, culturally, economically, intellectually, morally and spiritually transformed nation. This 18% of the population are individuals who are in communities, institutions, churches, businesses, governments and civil society. My view in this book is that if they are those whose relationships with God, self, fellow humans and the environment are restored, they can become changed minds and lives capable of changing people and places. For a person is truly changed when her or his inner person – will, emotion and intellect – is changed. Positive change of these human faculties enables a person to possess a transformed mind, overcome evil and stand for and promote the common good. The chief consequence of changing one's mind is the change of one's perspectives on divine-human and human-human relationships, which results in what I call revitalized moral agency.

REVITALIZED MORAL AGENCY

Good Governance

How can we achieve revitalized moral agency in Ethiopia, which enables us to achieve the common good, which is enabled through good governance or good political practices?

Good road networks and bridges; public transportation, parks, museums, schools and health systems; and enduring cultural values, civil liberties and protection of safety and security can all be seen as examples of the common good. All these in Ethiopia can be rated as poor or unsatisfactory. Lack of good political practices results in failing to achieve the common good and the vicious cycle of failure continues. This is compounded by the fact that bad governance ushers in the demise of government. Bad political practices ushered in the demise of the monarchy and then the military-communist regime. EPRDF's failure to address the problem of corruption and bad political practices ushered in its demise in 2019. Moral failure leads to political failure and then the end of a regime along with its system of governance.

This vicious cycle of failure has hampered efforts to build sustainable peace, democratic culture, unity-in-diversity and fair society. During the EPRDF era, for example, political power became absolute power and corrupted even good people absolutely. Absolute political power enabled EPRDF-related corporations to thrive, while existing state-owned corporations and private businesses weakened. Some individuals and firms that had good relations with the EPRDF government were able to use the state to their own advantage. These individuals were enabled to gain access to public officials and some organs of the state. In order to tackle these kinds of corrupt governance and illicit economic relationships, a critical mass of people with integrity and moral authority will need to be developed. These people can become moral agents, who stand for the common good and promote fundamental societal values.

SHALOM

The English term "peace" is the translation of the Hebrew *shalom* and Greek *eirene*. The Biblical term *shalom* is not only the absence of interstate wars or interethnic conflicts. Nor is it only the absence of social or familial strife or individual physical infirmities. *Shalom* means wholeness or completeness. For Biblical writers, *shalom* represents a cosmic order, security, wholeness and prosperity, so it is associated with God himself. The Greek *eirene* has a meaning of peace between individuals and communities and national tranquility. In Greek mythology, *Eirene* (Peace) was a Greek goddess. She is depicted in art as a beautiful young woman wearing a cloak, carrying a young child, holding a scepter in her right hand and carrying a symbol of abundance in her left arm. Ethiopia needs both *shalom* and *eirene*.

Ethiopia has suffered the absence of peace for so long due to internal and external conflicts. Since the 19th century, Ethiopia has fought with Britain, Italy (2x), Egypt, Sudan and Somalia. The country has suffered countless numbers of internal warfare. Between 1961 and 1991, multiple rebel forces fought against the Ethiopian government, the most notable being the Eritrean and Tigrean People's Liberation Fronts. Both forces, along with others, defeated the military-communist regime, and Eritrea gained independence, but peace did not return to Ethiopia. In fact, five years after Eritrea gained independence, Ethiopia and Eritrea fought a bloody border war. For 20 years, Eritrea and Ethiopia remained enemies. Enmity between people groups and political parties has existed within Ethiopia too. All this is because peace as a value has not gone hand-in-hand with forgiveness, reconciliation, truth, love, justice, etc.

Indeed, for three decades, the EPRDF tried to rule Ethiopia by preaching peace and development, without justice. It branded those who sought justice and fairness in politics and economics as anti-peace and anti-development forces. This resulted in political crisis. Mounting political pressure forced then Prime Minister Haile-Mariam Desalegn to launch the so-called "deep political reform agenda" within the EPRDF. He also accepted the proposal from religious leaders that a nation-wide process of peace building, forgiveness and reconciliation must be initiated. He wanted to build a national consensus that would lead the country toward national healing. But forces within the Tigray People's Liberation Front (TPLF), which politically dominated the EPRDF for almost three decades, prevented him from succeeding. This deepened the political crisis, which was further exacerbated by a tactical alliance formed by the Oromo and Amhara groups within the party against the TPLF. All this compelled Haile-Mariam to adopt a political strategy, whereby in February 2018 he resigned his position as prime minister and played a decisive role in having Abiy Ahmed elected as his successor in April 2018.

A year after Abiy Ahmed assumed power, the EPRDF's ideology of revolutionary democracy, which is rooted in Marxism-Leninism and to which the TPLF is absolutely committed, was replaced with a political system that claims to be combining political principles and values with Ethiopian social and cultural realities. Prime Minister Abiy also appeared to express dissatisfaction with a system of ethnic federalism, which had been masterminded by the TPLF. Although Abiy continued to claim to be committed to a federalist system, the

TPLF and other ethno-nationalist forces sought to maintain the status quo and accused Abiy of intending to bring about a unitarian system of governance. Their accusation was intensified when Abiy persuaded the majority within the party leadership to reform the party, although the matter had been in discussion well before Abiy came to power. This reform, for example, included change of the structure of the party, and its name from 'Ethiopian People's Revolutionary Democratic Front' (EPRDF) to 'Prosperity Party'. It also included partner-parties in Afar, Gambela, Somali and Benshangul-Gumuz regional administrations becoming full members with full rights and responsibilities. The previous policy would not have allowed any of these regions to nominate a candidate for the position of prime minister, for example, which was rightly regarded as unjust. All that changed.

Following these and many changes, the TPLF left the party altogether and many officials who served in various national military and civil leadership positions went back to Mekelle, the capital of the Tigray region. There was a relationship breakdown between the Tigray regional government and the federal government. Many attempts made by different groups to bring reconciliation between the TPLF and the federal government failed. In the meantime, the TPLF strengthened its regional special forces estimated to be over 300,000 strong. It then rejected the postponement in 2020 of the national elections due to the COVID-19 pandemic and held its own regional election in September 2020, which was judged unconstitutional and illegal by the Federal Parliament and House of Federation. In October 2020, the TPLF declared Abiy Ahmed's government illegal and ordered its members to leave their parliamentary seats and different ministerial positions at the federal level.

Then, something extraordinary happened. On November 4, 2020 at around 11 p.m. local time, Tigray regional forces, along with federal army members loyal to the TPLF attacked the unsuspecting Northern Command of the Ethiopian Federal Defence Forces stationed in different military bases in Tigray, took some of the Command's military equipment, detained thousands of its members and killed hundreds in horrific circumstances. Tigray officials admitted their forces carried out this pre-emptive attack, one of them describing it as a "thunder-like action" intended to demobilize the Northern Command and use its weapons to cripple the federal government.

The Ethiopian government saw all this as a treasonous act and carried out what it called "a law enforcement operation," which in actual fact was an all-out war. The TPLF was defeated. Many of those who planned and executed the attack against the federal forces for their egocentric and extremist political and economic goals were either killed or captured, but thousands of young and old lost their lives, millions of people in Tigray were left in desperate need of help, and this poor nation is once again scarred and divided needing urgent and deep national healing.

War is utterly undesirable, but I hope that pursuant to St. Augustine's principle, the Ethiopian government did not "seek peace in order to be at war," but it went to war in order to bring all warring parties to the prosperity of peace and that Ethiopia may have lasting peace. While it is true that sometimes justice may need to be served, justice without the spirit of forgiveness does not achieve peace. We cannot declare peace at all costs; nor can we affirm justice at all costs. Nor can we preach forgiveness, love or reconciliation at all costs.

It is so uncomfortable and complex. It is much easier to adopt justice without forgiveness, or truth without love or peace without reconciliation. But this easy approach is a wrong approach. Hard choices will need to be made to restore broken relationships caused by selfishness, violence, domination and exploitation. Peace accompanied with all other values is needed in Ethiopia. But to achieve peace, Ethiopians must talk to each other and listen to one another with humanity and humility. As Meaza Mengiste said in the *London Review of Books* titled 'Ethiopia's Long War':

Everything is at stake in discussions of Ethiopia's political present; not only our future, but our past. What might justice look like? At such a volatile moment, it seems impossible – and naïve – to plead for multilateral discussions, to imagine the potential benefits of negotiation. Yet it is difficult to conceive of another way forward that does not, sooner or later, include more bloodshed. Dialogue would be an unprecedented response to conflict in a nation that has built its identity on confrontation and conquest. It would require the audacity and the optimism of Abiy's early rule. It would require hope and the willingness and courage to delve into the past. Otherwise, what do we do with all that history – all that rage, all these memories? A young soldier with a slender face. Bruised and beaten men in the back of a truck. The site of a prison, a plaque on a wall. A new conflict shrouded in silence. The question is not where to begin, but how.

Ethiopia needs *shalom*; true peace between individuals and communities. For that to happen, however, all Ethiopians must declare in unison *Shabbat shalom*, which is how Jews greet each other on Friday evening before celebrating Sabbath on Saturday. The meaning of Sabbath (Shabbat) is to do with stopping.

Ethiopia's hope lies in its citizens' commitment to break the vicious cycle of confrontation, enmity and violence once and for all and pass *shalom* to the next generation.

TRUTH-SENSITIVE MENTALITY

That truth and truthfulness must be at the heart of any engagement within a democratic constitutional state is a given. But do all state officials, governmental and non-governmental organizations, and even ecclesiastical institutions place an enormous value on truth? The answer is "no" and a culture that tolerates half-truth, lies and deceptions seems to be developing. This unfortunately sustains the already existing vicious cycle of moral failure. So, Ethiopians must develop truth-sensitive mentality and apply that in religion and statecraft.

There was a rather provocative declaration in the *New York Times* (*The Age of Post-Truth Politics*, August 2016) that we are now living in a "post-truth democracy." The author of the article based his argument on the fact that 70% of Donald Trump's "factual" statements made during his presidential campaign actually fell into the categories of "mostly false", "false" and lies. The *Washington Post* (January 2021) recently reported that Trump's false or misleading claims total 30,573 over four years. A White House Official once defended him by referring to a false claim as "alternative facts" and Rudy Giuliani declared that "truth isn't truth." All this, coupled with leaders and advisors with a questionable relationship with the truth occupying the British government and 10 Downing Street, might give the impression that we are now living in a post-truth democracy.

However, these worst examples do not change the fact that

Western democracies regard truth as the foundation of every-thing, including freedom and democracy. Freedom founded on lies is not freedom. Democracy in the absence of ethical and moral values is not democracy. Democratic states will always take the supremacy of the law seriously. And the supremacy of the law demands the centrality of truth. So, post-truth democracy would not be a democracy. For democracy to be true democracy in Ethiopia, therefore, ethics and moral values must play a greater role in political discussions, policy-making and setting the vision for the direction of the nation.

Ethiopians must have a conviction that truth is the founda-tion of family, society, church, nation and the world and, there-fore, should never be violated. Furthermore, with sensitivity, neutrality, love and humility, Ethiopians in general and religious institutions in particular should always call out misuse of truth or misleading use of facts and figures by political or religious leaders, whatever the cost. As morality is an inescapable part of public life and cannot simply be reduced to private preferences, politicians who show disregard for truth and promote false-hood must be challenged. No politician, including the prime minister and president, should be immune from criticism for failure to take the centrality of truth seriously. For if religious institutions fail to champion the truth, truth as the founda-tional ethical value will suffer in society and societal integrity as a whole will be in danger. So, the role of truth-centered ethics in politics and economics must be paramount in Ethiopia's future.

ETHICAL ECONOMY

In the West, people are led to believe that happiness is the supreme good. Wealth through selfishness and greed is also believed to bring about happiness. As a result, morality in both politics and the economy is undermined. Religion is strictly privatized, which has led to the privatization of morality. This has undermined fidelity and commitment in relationships and public life. It has also undermined trust and fairness in economic relationships. Now, the West is battling to recover the principle of building a successful economy on trust and fairness.

Ethiopian politicians and the business community must learn from the West. They need to understand that while the principle of free market economics may enable and encourage wealth creation, much work needs to be done to actually make it free and fair. Most importantly, it has to have all the core values at its center. So, the Ethiopian government's task must be devising mechanisms and creating conducive environments for creating wealth in a free, fair and equitable manner. Furthermore, it is crucial that the government ensures that the market does not rule and that there is morality in it. To achieve this, it is highly desirable for the government to be influenced by those who take the moral principles of trust, trustworthiness, fairness, and neighbor-love seriously. If these principles underpin the statecraft, the market will not rule Ethiopia.

Also, Ethiopian politicians must always bear in mind that there is morality in wealth creation. Even Adam Smith, the Scottish Enlightenment writer who famously said that there was no morality in markets, argued that frugality, honesty and duty facilitated a good economy and underpinned a good society. Poverty, ignorance and all the social ills that have dogged Ethiopia for centuries cannot be properly addressed without an effective system of wealth creation. Former British Prime

Minister Margaret Thatcher was known for advocating the morality of wealth creation. She famously said that "no one would remember the Good Samaritan if he'd only had good intentions; he had money as well." It is true that the Good Samaritan could not have saved the deserted and dying man if he had not had two things: compassion and money. So she was right. The main problem with her government was that she appeared to be heartless towards those who were losing their jobs. She also let the market rule, as it set all the standards and her government imposed little or no regulations.

As markets were basically uncontrolled entities driven by selfishness and greed, they caused huge damage. In the world of the markets, principles of truth, fairness and trust were seen as less important than material comforts. Market principles encouraged people to buy things they did not need and with money they did not have. They would buy beautiful cars, homes and luxury items on credit, which is part of what Yuval Harari, in his *Sapiens*, calls "imagined realities" or "collective fictions" which guide the social behavior of humans and on which modern systems are built. Credit is used to buy things in order to buy happiness, which does not last for very long. But this, as the late Chief Rabbi Jonathan Sacks has often pointed out, is done in the context where morals are outsourced to markets, whose growth is driven largely by the principle of credit.

Hope for Ethiopia lies in promoting ethical economy, at the heart of which are fidelity, fairness and sacrificial sharing of resources. This can be achieved if a critical mass of transformed individuals is at the forefront in terms of promoting ethical economy in all sectors of society. It can be achieved if the government is committed to prioritizing the most vulnerable in society by adopting the principle of social justice alongside the policy of wealth creation. Then, free market economics in Ethiopia will become a vehicle through which a fairer and better society is created.

RECONSIDERED IDENTITY

I proposed earlier that in order to reach the 18% minority whose transformed opinion could tip the opinion of the majority towards bringing about sustainable change in Ethiopia, a process of multiplication or regeneration is to be adopted. In this process, our understanding of problems of identity must be central. The term "identity" belongs to a group of social-categorization terminologies. I would like to discuss here religious, racial, ethnic and national identities briefly. For religious identities in Ethiopia, I will use Christian identity as an example.

IDENTITIES

Let me start with Christian identity in Ethiopia. In the ancient religious world, Christians were probably understood as a distinct race or people while maintaining their Jewish, Greek or Roman identities. But Christians did not have a hybrid identity. Indeed, in the early periods as a whole, we cannot find any evidence where ethnic identities were fused so as to create a hybrid identity; nor was the notion of ethnic identities being transcended by one particular identity conceivable at the time. In any case, when we talk about Christian identity in Ethiopia, we are talking about the Ethiopian Catholic identity, the Ethiopian Orthodox identity and the Ethiopian Protestant-evangelical identity.

First, the Ethiopian Catholic Church shares in the ancient

Ethiopian Christian heritage, which goes back to St. Frumentius, who in the 4th century AD started Christianity in Ethiopia and later served as the first bishop of the Church of Ethiopia. This shared heritage should be understood as continuing until the split between the Church of Rome and Orthodox Churches in 1054 AD. Indeed, until this fateful year, there was one "catholic" or universal church in the world. Thereafter, attempts that were made to reestablish the bond between the Roman Catholic Church and the Ethiopian Orthodox Church were unsuccessful.

But as Empress Eleni had already established a diplomatic relationship between Portugal (a Catholic nation) and Ethiopia, Emperor Galawdewos (1540-1559) forged an alliance with the Portuguese to fight jihadist Islam. Then Jesuit missionaries in the early 17th century succeeded in converting Emperor Zadengel (1603-1604). Consequently, Zedengel's successor, Emperor Susenyos (1607-1632), declared Catholicism as the state religion. This resulted in a civil war, which caused the death of thousands and much destruction. It also resulted in the abdication of the king himself and the expulsion of all Catholic missionaries. It was two centuries later that Catholic missionaries were able to set foot in Ethiopia. Nowadays, there are almost a million Catholics in the country.

Second, the Ethiopian Orthodox Tewahedo Church (EOTC) is the largest Christian denomination in Ethiopia with about 40 million members. The EOTC sees itself as the custodian of the early Christian heritage. While the EOTC could be seen as part of worldwide Catholic Christianity until the division in 1054 AD, since the 5th century AD it aligned itself with the so-called Oriental Orthodox Churches in Egypt, Syria, Armenia and India more than churches in the East or West.

This was because of the creed formulated by the Council of Chalcedon in 451 AD, which defined the doctrine of Christ.

For centuries, the head of the EOTC was sent from the Coptic Church in Egypt. But since 1950, the EOTC has been appointing its own patriarch. As indicated elsewhere, the Ethiopian Orthodox Church was the state church of Ethiopia from the beginning of Christianity until 1974. While the EOTC is part of the family of Oriental Orthodox Churches, it has unique elements in its tradition and practices such as one or more of the replica of the Ark of the Covenant housed in each church, *Mesqel* (the finding of the true cross), and *T'imqet* (Ethiopian epiphany).

Third, Protestant-evangelical denominations make up 20% of the Ethiopian population. They include all movements within evangelicals, Pentecostals and charismatics that stand in the traditions of the Protestant Reformation. Protestantism has been in Ethiopia for just over a century.

While Ethiopian Catholic, Orthodox and Protestant-evangelical Christians are doctrinally divided, they have a shared identity on the following grounds. First, they are Gentile Christians, who are counted as part of the children of Abraham. Second, as in 1 Peter, they can be referred to as a race, i.e. a universal community of people, although their new identity as a new creation or race is different from their racial, ethnic or national identities. Fourth, all three traditions share the belief in the doctrine of Trinity and in Jesus as the Son of God. Fifth, all three traditions accept the Nicene Creed, which declares, "[We believe] in one holy Catholic and apostolic Church." Sixth, all Catholics, Orthodox and Protestant-evangelicals in Ethiopia are sharers of the early Christian heritage that began in the 4th century AD. Finally, all Catholics, Orthodox and

Protestant-evangelicals are sharers of the national narrative of Ethiopia as a nation-state. Members of these denominations are at once members of an ethnic group, citizens of Ethiopia, part of the universal community of Christians and members of the global human family.

Christian identity is different from racial identity, which is to do with a group of people with similar physical characteristics. There are some who believe that *race* is the primary determinant of human capacities and that individuals should be treated differently according to their race. This belief is rejected nowadays. So is any kind of discrimination on the basis of simply belonging to "another" group, which is seen as unrelated to "our" group. Racial identity is not as big an issue in Ethiopia as it is in the West, but we cannot say the same about ethnic identity.

Ethnic identity is to do with socio-cultural norms, customs, traditions and shared memory that connect members of a people group. In the Ethiopian context, ethnic identity may be based on shared past or culture, but that shared past or culture may not always be real. That is to say, ethnic identity may not always be based on an indisputable ancestral origin and shared past. It may simply be imagined or invented and then given socio-political shape and form. In any case, the notion is rooted in the fact that humans are preoccupied with vitality and its origins, which makes them seek to form relations around those origins. People groups with shared kinship as well as common language and shared memory would naturally attempt to move towards self-determination, which starts at family and clan levels. In order to protect and preserve family, parents put the wellbeing of their children before their own. Similarly, a clan puts the wellbeing of its own sets of families before members of other clans. A tribe or an ethnic group puts the wellbeing of its members before others. These family-clan-tribe structures are provided territorial definition, which naturally demands self-determination.

However, the claim of being a people and sharing an ancestry has brought with it the problem of knowing where to draw the boundary. In the Ethiopian context, this has also brought with it the problem of knowing what to do about other people groups who live side by side with a people group that shares a real or imagined/invented ancestry. What is even more problematic is the fact that in recent decades ethnic identity has been explained in terms of an ethnic group viewing its identity outside of the history of the state of Ethiopia. This has led some to focus on their group's beliefs, practices and institutions and operate within the categories of "us" versus "them." This, coupled with the notion of self-determination, has become a huge problem particularly in relation to national identity.

National identity is Ethiopian identity. It is to do with belonging to the Ethiopian state based on sharing a common land with common borders and laws and having a shared narrative developed over centuries. By Ethiopia, I mean the present political and geographical nation-state of Ethiopia. Ancient Ethiopia was known as *Cush, Sheba* or *Aithiopis*. We cannot know with any degree of certainty how much of the land and which groups of people of the present Ethiopia were part of that ancient state. But we can know that Ethiopia's singular nationhood came about when different people groups shared a common land together with common borders; accepted ideals believed to transcend differences without dissolving certain particularities; associated themselves with shared historical and cultural values and aspirations; developed national consciousness; and committed themselves to a shared national identity under a shared narrative of *Ethiopianness*.

This sense of *national identity* is deeply embedded in the societal psyche that it becomes almost unconscious. Ethiopianness is an inner passion for the country and its people, and an emotional bond with this mystical *Motherland*. Through music, arts, sport, a national anthem and invoking common causes and symbols, this passion is rekindled and commitment to the shared identity and history is renewed. This sense of national identity has sustained the Ethiopian state for centuries. But in contemporary Ethiopia, ethnic identity is pitted against national identity. Indeed, according to the current Constitution of Ethiopia, which seeks to marry ethnic diversity with federalism, ethnic identity is given precedence over national identity and all other identities. So the State of the Federal Democratic Republic of Ethiopia is made up of regional states that are sovereign but are "voluntarily" federated to each other. This primacy of ethnic identity has encouraged the act of fusing ethnic and religious identities, as a result of which the integrity of the country as a nation-state is threatened.

FUSION OF ETHNIC AND RELIGIOUS IDENTITIES

Ethnic or national identity can be fused with any religious identity. This is true in Ethiopia. For example, many understand Orthodox Tewahido Christianity as the foundation of their ethno-nationalist and personal identity. So, an Ethiopian born and brought up in Gondar or Lalibela or Axum would understand herself or himself as someone who cannot be anything other an Orthodox Tewahido Christian. This leads to the belief that political processes must center on the fusion of

Amhara or Tigre identity with Tewahido faith. This is unambiguously illustrated by Prof Getachew Haile's famous declaration:

"I used to believe that I love the *Tewahido* Christianity because it is the Orthodox or the right faith. I do not believe that any more. I believe that I love my church – which happens to be the true Church of Christ – because it is mine, like my mother, my father, my wife, my children and like my country … The truth, therefore, lies not in who is in the right and who is in the wrong, but in who is born where."[38]

Getachew does not claim that he is Amhara or Tigre but for him it is clear that "who he is" cannot be divorced from his *Tewahido* Christianity because he was born in it. I call this fusion of ethnic/national identity and religious identity. Such an approach was widely accepted during the monarchic rule in Ethiopia, as Ethiopian Orthodox *Tewahido* Christianity was both religion and state with the Emperor as the *Defender of the Faith*.

Nowadays, some Oromos believe that political processes must center on the fusion of ethnic identity (plus some sort of territoriality) with Islam and/or their ancestral religious tradition called *Waaqa* (or *Waaqeffannaa*). For some radical Muslim Oromos, a true Oromo is a Muslim. This is also true for many in the Muslim-dominated Somali and Afar regions. Such an approach is consistent with the ways in which Islam was introduced in the Middle East, where it became both religion and state. Furthermore, other people groups in Ethiopia are trying to go back, with a huge political backing, to their real or imagined roots and develop traditions that fuse their ethnic identity with their ancestral religio-cultural identity. In ancient and modern times, similar approaches have resulted in religious and political extremism.

Ethnic identity directly appeals to shared descent, history, territory, language, cult and customs. Religion is a matter of conscience and personal choice or persuasion and cannot be seen as something inextricably linked with a particular ethnic group. As it would be wrong to say that all people from a specific ethnic group should be socialists or neo-liberals, so also would it be wrong to claim that a certain religion is a given to a certain people group or humanity as a whole was born with a certain religion. Nationalistic or ethnocentric rhetoric that fuses ethnic and religious identities could easily garner deep loyalties with potentially irrational foundations, which, if not countered by rational arguments, could lead to *negative* "us" versus "them" polarizations and then to conflicts and human misery.

Indeed, as Lamin Sanneh has rightly argued, in contemporary Africa, the politicization of religion and ethnicity has diminished the contribution that religion and ethnic diversity can make in bringing moral and ethical values into the public square. Consequently, society has been deprived of moral leadership, communities of faith have been marginalized, and neighborliness has suffered. Sanneh further argues that ethnic division and religious fundamentalism are 'a sop to political manipulation: they accentuate the divisions that hinder our capacity for mutual charity and forbearance; they make governance dysfunctional and society divided'.[39] This is true of the contemporary Ethiopian situation.

I, therefore, argue that claims in Ethiopia that people from a certain ethnic group should be Orthodox, Catholic, Muslim or Protestant must be wholly rejected. Political processes that center, for example, on the fusion of the Amhara or Tigrean identity with Orthodox Tewahido Christianity or the Oromo identity with Islam and/or *Waaqeffannaa* or the Hadiya identity with Protestantism (or some traditional religion) are good neither for politics nor religion. While the misinterpretations of the constitutional separation of state and religion need to be corrected, we must continue to support the idea of a secular state guided by the principles of democracy, freedom and equality.

REDESIGNED STATECRAFT

THE POLITICS OF *MEDEMER*

In April 2018, when the country was on the verge of disintegration, Dr. Abiy Ahmed was elected as prime minister and introduced the term *medemer* into the Ethiopian political discourse. He also wrote a book with the same title. The term literally means "to be added up", but it has been translated as "synergy." Synergy, which is used in philosophy, technology, business and politics, means an interaction or cooperation between two or more beings, agents, actors or organizations in order to produce a combined effect that is greater than the sum of their separate effects. From reading his book, one can understand that Dr. Abiy came up with this idea because he came to believe that a clear-cut emphasis on socio-anthropological or ideological paradigms that set the individual against the community, ethno-nationalism against civic nationalism, conservatism against liberalism, or capitalism against socialism are at best simplistic, at worst an impossibility. So he seeks to introduce a new framework in Ethiopian statecraft. Abiy's

Medemer, I think, is an important contribution to an ongoing conversation regarding the journey and destiny of Ethiopia as a nation-state made up of diverse people groups. I wish to start my discussion in this section by analyzing this book.

MEDEMER: ANALYSIS

Dr. Abiy proposed the politics of *medemer* as the only solution to the dangerously developing political situation under the government of the Ethiopian People's Revolutionary Democratic Front (EPRDF), which had sought to adopt the principles and practices of "revolutionary democracy" or, as it was later called, "developmental democracy." Many have concluded that the current problems resulted, by and large, from the EPRDF's overemphasis on ethnic diversity and a radical approach that sought to marry ethnicity with federalism.

In his book, Dr. Abiy's argument starts with the innate human need for self-preservation, self-defense, freedom and protecting one's name or honor. These needs are directly linked with issues of identity, because demand for recognition of identity is tantamount to demand for elevation of one's name or honor. Dr. Abiy argues that it is preferable and indeed more helpful to synergize these needs rather than rigidly sequencing them in the order of their pre-supposed importance. This principle, for Dr. Abiy, also applies to the polarized notions of "nature" and "nurture" as determinants of human destiny. That is to say, neither predestined nature nor environmentally determined and free-will-based nurture can independently determine human destiny. In Dr. Abiy's view, the same would be true about political philosophies.

So, Abiy would argue, neither liberalism with its emphasis

on the individual, small government and free market economics nor socialism with its emphasis on worker-centered and state-run economic systems could survive on its own. Furthermore, neither neo-liberalism with its revised attempt to embed limited government intervention and economic justice in free-market capitalism nor social democracy with its revised attempt to embed social justice and state intervention in free market economics has provided lasting solutions towards human development. Dr. Abiy admits that the EPRDF, with its socialist roots, sought to move towards social democracy by using revolutionary democracy as a bridge, but he argues that the EPRDF's ideology failed to achieve this.

By way of explaining this failure, he levels several criticisms against the EPRDF. First, it held a principle that set the individual and state in tension: the former is seen as selfish while the latter as an entity that manages fair wealth distribution. The EPRDF portrayed its political elites (revolutionary scholars), who led the state bureaucratic machinery, as unselfish, enlightened and committed to the common people. But in actual fact, they were corrupt, and known for rent collection and mismanagement, so the EPRDF's principles and claims contradicted its practices. Second, the EPRDF held a misguided belief that all human problems could be solved through economic development and, in so doing, ignored needs that distinguish humans from other animals, namely freedom, justice, equality, etc. Third, its policy of implementing the principles of developmental state and moving Ethiopia towards prosperity was hampered due to direct state involvement in the market, which created fat-cats from within the EPRDF while systematically pushing non-EPRDF wealth-creators out of the market. Fourth, the party violated the Constitution by deliberately narrowing the political space and governing the country under a one-party system. Fifth, while the EPRDF's focus on a peasant-centered economy is necessary, it failed to fully apply capitalist strategies of economic outputs. Sixth, it sought to establish a strong party rather than strong state bureaucracy assisted by independent, impartial and apolitical civil, judicial and democratic institutions. As a result of all this, in Dr. Abiy's view, the EPRDF experienced terminal illness endangering Ethiopia's future. So he presents the philosophy of *medemer* as a solution, if not universal panacea.

Medemer, for Dr. Abiy, is an art of producing political and economic resources by bringing together existing internal values and combining them with external capabilities. This, in his view, not only addresses Ethiopia's national loneliness, which has resulted in national decay, but it also enables its citizens to work toward a common goal of creating common identity and to take initiatives based on relationships. Through these foundational elements, central values of national unity and citizens' dignity can be reinforced. In order to achieve this sort of synergy, however, extremist, nostalgic, simplistic, scornful, lazy and pretentious attitudes must be challenged. Dr. Abiy further argues that in order to safeguard trust and relationships in society, red lines must be drawn against practices that reward inefficiency rather than competence and that are void of conscience, characterized by tolerating evil forces and a disregard for justice.

By proposing solutions, Dr. Abiy argues that we must create a system where citizens are no longer treated as second-class or even aliens; where the few could not wield absolute power; and where freedom, equality and democratic rights are not suppressed. In order to create such a system, however, "human-

and structure-born oppressions" must be removed. The notions of liberty and equality must go together with the notion of fraternity, which currently is weak due to ethnic-based competition and the lack of civic culture. Developing civic culture includes not only replacing the "ruler" culture with the "leader" culture but also synergizing the ideologically-polarized civic nationalism, which focuses on the individual, against ethnic nationalism, which focuses on a group. This synergizing process requires critical and scholarly examination of existing ideas through patient and participatory consultative engagements. Through augmenting these engagements with national peace and reconciliation efforts, Dr. Abiy hopes, defeating extremist forces on the one hand and creating a system that keeps Ethiopia's diverse ethnic groups together as a single economic, social and political community on the other could be achieved.

Dr. Abiy, however, understands that this cannot be sustained without building a democratic culture undergirded by basic international values. Nor can it be achieved without addressing macro-economic problems by synergizing the legal, standardizing and regulatory roles of the government with the roles of private enterprises, international investors, civil societies and educational institutions under the principles of free-market economics and fair-play. This process must necessarily include fair wealth distribution, a knowledge-led economic system and technological development, as well as synergizing a developmental state and the market. It must also include regional integration and healthy foreign policy, which are based on the principles of patriotism, protecting national interest through fostering friendship rather than antipathy, reconciling cooperation with competition, etc. All this will contribute to regional peace and development. It will also contribute to the internal growth of the export market, the effort of job creation and achieving food security for the growing population.

APPRAISAL OF *MEDEMER*

As he himself admits, Dr. Abiy's *Medemer* is not an academic work and in places it is rambling and repetitive. For the first time reader, he might seem to border on holding idealized views that cannot be translated into reality. He, for example, rejects a foreign policy that centers on the principle of "no permanent friend or enemy" and seeks to embrace a policy that is based on the absence of a "foe versus friend" principle. While this is highly desirable for any peace-loving Ethiopian, one might rightly wonder if such a policy would work in reality in this dangerous world. Dr. Abiy, however, has an acute awareness of the complexity of the issues he deals with, so he consistently attempts to critically weigh one option against another. His arguments take historical and contextual realities into account and seek to offer perspectives that, as he sees them, are balanced. As he was part of the EPRDF system, his critical appraisal of his own party in such a scathing manner raised a few eyebrows, but his brutally honest insider's assessment should be applauded and seen as exemplary.

The book, however, does not deal with issues relating to state and religion in any meaningful way. Nor does it deal with matters relating to gender in the Ethiopian context. Dr. Abiy's political ideology seems to embrace, wittingly or unwittingly, Anthony Giddens' "third-way" politics, which sought to marry globalization with nation-state and free-market economics or successful business with social justice. This idea, which influenced politicians such as Tony Blair, Bill Clinton and Gordon

Brown, developed out of the so-called "structuration" theory, which sought to resolve the competing views of structure (societal institutions) and agency (individual expression of will) by showing how they interface with one another. But there is not a single work of Giddens' in his bibliography.[40] Dr. Abiy, however, must be commended for his attempt to offer a fresh political framework.

When Dr. Abiy introduced the politics of *medemer* in 2018, many understood it as counter-narrative to the EPRDF ideology of ethnic federalism and indeed as a declaration of a unitarian system. However, what he means by *medemer* is synergizing internal values and external capacities; past history and present realities; civic nationalism and ethnic nationalism with a focus on patriotism; neo-liberalism and social democracy based on contextual veracities; individual rights and group rights; cooperation and competition with foreign nations, etc.

ADDITIONAL SUGGESTIONS

While we are acutely aware of the complexity of our world, it is probably safe to argue that simplified and polarized frameworks cannot address Ethiopia's intricate ethno-religious and political problems. Ethiopia's situation demands a new framework that synergizes opposing or competing frameworks and takes into account an honest assessment of Ethiopia's historical and contextual realities. Hence, Dr. Abiy's attempt is to be commended.

To make some additional suggestions, first, we need to realize that ethno-nationalism along with the notion of self-determination is a 20th century phenomenon. And the claim of being a people and sharing an ancestry has brought with it the problem of knowing where to draw the boundary. In the Ethiopian context, this has also brought with it the problem of knowing what to do to other people groups who live side by side with a people group that shares a real or imagined/invented ancestry. The principle of majority rule and minority right has been proposed as a solution. Some radicals might even propose the notion of annihilation, expulsion or total assimilation as a solution. Neither has worked. I would insist that Ethiopia's common narrative about shared identity and uniting symbols should be strengthened, creating a society where no one is superior or subservient and the principle of equal opportunity and meritocracy is supreme.

Second, our ethnography and geography must be reconsidered. The world was designed in such a way that the limitation of the ethnographical and geographical horizons can be transcended. It is true that in the historical context of Ethiopia, family-clan-tribe structures had territorial definition with multiple autonomous chiefdoms. Scholars often contrast this with the project of the unitarian system arguably implemented during the era of Emperor Haile-Selassie. Some argue that this system was exclusive, as it was characterized by the hegemony of the Amhara (e.g. Donald Levine). Others argue that it was inclusive, as it was characterized by the dominance of the Orthodox Christian religion and Amharic language (e.g. Christopher Clapham). Still others argue that Ethiopia always was an ethnocratic state and pan-Ethiopianism was never achieved, as the imperial state was a loose conglomeration of ethnic groups with their own geographical boundaries.[41]

A rigid choice of one or the other has prevented us from moving beyond the current cul-de-sac, enabling radical ethnocentric hermeneutic and geography to be articulated rather vociferously. While geographical contexts may be necessary, there cannot be geographical center and geographical periphery. While family-clan-tribe structures are a reality, there cannot be ethnographical center and ethnographical periphery. While the constitutional provision of the right to self-government of each people group may be useful, we must accept that in today's Ethiopia, the principle of "majority rule" and "minority right" has turned into a practice of tyranny of the majority and disenfranchisement of the minority. The viability of a radical ethnocentric hermeneutic, ethnocentric geography and ethnically organized government must be reconsidered.

Third, the concept of national sovereignty – as against the notion of multiple sovereign nations within one nation-state – has to be strengthened. Self-rule and the absence of occupation by foreigners define national sovereignty. I would agree with Kwame Appiah that national sovereignty is a political tenet that commands audible assent.[42] But assent to national sovereignty is different from nationalism, which, against the Enlightenment rationalism, focused on people's language and culture as uniting elements. This vision of a nation united by language and culture is in tension with the reality of linguistic and cultural variation within the same nation. So the focus must be on a sovereign nation-state with different languages, cultural expressions and origins but united through sharing the same land, being under a single national government, sharing common language, common cultural values and common history and symbols. National sovereignty depends on developed national consciousness. But as Appiah argues, national consciousness is not a mineral to be excavated but a fabric to be woven. In this case, national territorial integrity is more important than self-determination, which, at the moment, is seen as a sacrosanct ideal in Ethiopia. In our context, national sovereignty must serve as a source of legitimacy more profoundly than self-determination driven by radical ethno-nationalist and ethno-religious agendas.

Fourth, if we prefer national sovereignty over against self-determination and multiple sovereignties without denying linguistic and cultural diversities, we must then consider the principle of ethno-cosmopolitan patriotism.[43] The ethno-cosmopolitan does not abandon ethnic identity and patriotic fervor but combines ethnic and patriotic commitments within a global perspective and seeks to counter evils of nationalism and ethnocentrism. The ethno-cosmopolitan patriot invests in the national honor and cares about her country's policies and actions. She lives with ambiguities rather than absolute certainties about her identity. She combines respect for her own culture and language with a respect for others' culture and language. She does not deny that humans are preoccupied with vitality and its origins and, as a result, seek to form relations around those origins. But she combines a sense of shared commitment with a relaxed sense that includes others who do not necessarily share a common ancestry or history or language. Through this, she is ready to challenge those who seek to destroy life in Ethiopia through venerating certainties about their identity and imagined past.

Finally, ethno-cosmopolitan patriotism gives priority to social cohesion and national sovereignty and seeks common understanding towards peace, love, truth and justice. It keeps the balance between the local and global identities while guided by the original pattern of universal kinship. It emphasizes a movement towards a universal identity based on the common origin, but it acknowledges cultural and religious diversity and, therefore, does not reject the particularity of communal loyalties. In order to prevent such loyalties from becoming extremist ideologies, I suggest that we should do three things. First, our government should adopt a policy that permits religious education in secondary schools and academic study of religions at universities in a manner that is free from promotion of religious dogmas. Second, we should foster ecumenical relationships within Christianity in order to enable Catholics, Orthodox and Protestants to speak with one voice about issues of common concern. Finally, we should introduce interreligious dialogue between Islam and Christianity in order to develop the culture of accommodating and mentally engaging with each other in the spirit of honesty and integrity and on the basis of the principle of respect for human dignity.

❧ 4 ❧

SECULAR STATE VERSUS
SECULARIST STATE

A religious state or state religion cannot be in the interest of Ethiopia with –according to the 2007 Census – 43.5% Orthodox, 33.9% Muslims, 0.7% Catholics, 18.6% Protestant-evangelicals and 2.7% adherents of traditional religions. Christians should stand for the idea of a secular state. By secular state, I am not talking about a state that exclusively follows secularist philosophy, which either rejects religion altogether or seeks to undermine religious belief while at the same time claiming to defend the right of individuals to have religious faith and liberty. Secular humanists also do not accept any religious expression in the political sphere and the contribution of religious values to societal moral progress.

As Lamin Sanneh has argued, Africa as a whole "has been the bearer of two massive and uneven influences, one secular and the other religious. The secular influence is entrenched in the autonomy of the sovereign nation-state, and the religious in the steady expansion of Christianity and Islam on the continent." These influences were introduced by colonial powers. Sanneh argues that in the post-colonial era, Africans have not had much opportunity for critical reflection on the African understanding of the relation of politics and religion. Consequently, a western understanding of the secular state was adopted, at least, by African elites. Sanneh proposed to his African colleagues the time was right to advance an African Christian understanding of the relation between church and state.[1]

Ethiopia was never colonized and, therefore, did not have colonial influences in terms of the dichotomization between the sacred and the secular. However, since the introduction of Marxism-Leninism in 1974 and 'revolutionary democracy' (another Marxist formula) in 1991, the situation became confused. So, following Sanneh's suggestion, I would argue that a new understanding of the relation between religion and state should be developed in Ethiopia. I would also argue that Ethiopia should remain a secular state.

But the secular state I am proposing does not endorse secularist ideals, but rather a state that is committed to democratic principles of justice, equity, peace, security and unity of its subjects, but has a place for the role of religion in the public square. This state can be founded on the principle of separation of religion and state as, for example, clearly enshrined in Article 11 of the Ethiopian Constitution. In a secular-democratic state, religion does not interfere in the affairs of the state and vice versa, but this does not necessarily mean that state and religion have nothing to do with each other. As Sanneh rightly argues, "the injunction about rendering to Caesar the things that are Caesar's, and to God the things that are God's conceals a subtle and much overlooked critical nexus about the things in which

God and Caesar are united, however unevenly, rather than in the things in which they are divided.'[2] As discussed earlier, it is regrettable that the Ethiopian government misguidedly thought that religion had nothing to do with the state and had no interest to hear any critical and constructive voice of religion. It is also unfortunate that some Christian communities dichotomized so sharply between the 'things of God' and the 'things of Caesar' that they believed that they had little or nothing to do with politics and the political state. As a result, until recently, religious values played no significant role towards moral and cultural progress of the country. That erroneous view has now changed, but the notion of secular state is maintained.

The notion begins with fully respecting Article 18 of the Universal Declaration of Human Rights, which reads: "Everyone has the right to freedom of thought, conscience and religion; this right includes freedom to change his religion or belief, and freedom, either alone or in community with others and in public or private, to manifest his religion or belief in teaching, practice, worship and observance." The article is adopted word for word in Article 27 of the Ethiopian Constitution along with clauses that provide for establishing institutions and organizations, legal protection for the believer, parental right to bring up their children within their religion and freedom to express one's religion while protecting the freedom of others. Ethiopians must reject any attempt that seeks to erode or replace Article 18, as was the case in The Cairo Declaration of Human Rights in Islam. Secular state guided by democratic principles and religious space is Ethiopia's future.

Along this line, first, a secular state fully recognizes the vital importance of religion in the public square. Second, a secular state ensures equality, where members of any religion or denomination would be treated as citizens with equal rights and obligations. Third, a secular state ensures security of religious adherents, who may be inherently vulnerable because of their unequivocal rejection of any kind of individually sanctioned or group-sponsored violent activities. In connection with this, fourth, in a secular state the monopoly of violence is only exercised by the State and its legally and legitimately established security structures in the context of accountability, fairness and justice. Fourth, a secular state ensures freedom. While the state guarantees the freedom of the individual and society, it also ensures that any freedom, including political and religious freedom, is subordinate to the rule of law. Finally, within a secular state, religious institutions must exercise the principles of accommodation of ethnic, religious and political differences, peaceful co-existence with one another and mutual respect.

5

DEMOCRATIC ELECTIONS IN ETHIOPIA

CONTEXTUAL BACKGROUND

For centuries, Ethiopia was ruled by a hereditary monarchic system that claimed its connection to Biblical Solomon. Such a claim was based on the story of the Queen of Sheba in 1 Kings 10, which is further developed by a document called *Kebre-Negest* ('The Glory of Kings'), which was first produced in Coptic probably in 6th century AD and then translated into Arabic and Ge'ez (with some embellishments) in 14th century AD.[1] In the Ge'ez version, the document compares the emperor of Rome with the emperor of Ethiopia. Both are sons of Solomon, but the emperor of Ethiopia was the first-born, whom the Queen bore to Solomon and who was appointed by God to reign in his earthly kingdom, the new Zion (Ethiopia). The document presents the new king of the New Zion as someone who plays the twin role of political leadership to bring order and cohesion into a lawless and fragmented nation and religious leadership to destroy paganism, spread Christianity and defend Orthodox Christian faith. Almost all Ethiopian emperors appealed to this "biblical" imperial past in order to legitimate their authority. They were, therefore, seen as part of the Solomonic dynasty, elects of God and replicas of the Heavenly King in the earthly kingdom of God.

That was precisely why Haile Selassie (1930-1974), the last Emperor of Ethiopia, bore such a long title: *The Conquering Lion of the Tribe of Judah, His Imperial Majesty Haile Selassie I, King of Kings of Ethiopia, Elect of God.* But Emperor Haile Selassie was the first to introduce a system of election in Ethiopia. The Constitution of Ethiopia, which was revised in 1955 under his oversight, provided for three crucial things: an elected chamber, a chamber of deputies appointed by the Emperor (the Senate) and an independent judiciary. It also provided for a ministerial government that was responsible to the monarch and parliament.

The power of the parliament made up of popularly elected representatives was balanced by the power of the Senate made up of the nobility and wealthy landlords. The Emperor was the head of state and government. He was also the head of the Ethiopian Orthodox Tewahido Church. In addition to all this, he oversaw the judiciary through his Crown Court. In his attempt to manage the inevitable competitions and political intrigues amongst these groups, Haile Selassie rendered himself ineffective. When the system failed to work, oppression and injustice increased, and discontent grew in all quarters, Haile Selassie attempted to decentralize and delegate power. But it was too little, too late, and the inevitable revolution led by the army and student movements broke out in 1974. This brought Haile-Selassie's 44 years' rule and the Ethiopian monarchy, along with its biblical claims, to an end. It also brought all the hopes of democratic processes to an end, as Marxism-Leninism became the guiding political principle of the country.

During the era of the Marxist-Leninist regime led by the Ethiopian Workers Party popularly known as the Dergue, representatives for the National Shengo were elected. But election in those days was not the process through which people expressed their will. The country was under a single party system. The Ethiopian Workers Party predetermined who should represent a given constituency. Names and pictures of candidates appeared in towns and villages. People were told to cast their votes on the election day and the "elected" candidates were declared. The whole operation was so undemocratic and utterly nonsensical. It was an insult to people's intelligence. People then gradually but quietly turned their backs on the regime, which hastened its demise.

After the end of the Dergue era in 1991, the EPRDF introduced a multi-party system. The first contested parliamentary and regional council elections took place in 2000. When the EPRDF encountered stiff opposition in some areas and realized that it was going to lose control, it sent in security forces to intimidate opposition supporters and their candidates. That inevitably created unrest and engendered resentment amongst the populace. Many opposition leaders were jailed with no credible charges against them. The EPRDF was declared the winner, but much of what happened, by and large, was utterly inconsistent with the spirit of democracy.

The 2005 election was different from the one in 2000, as it was highly contested and, by and large, reflected the main ingredients in democratic elections. The EPRDF was declared the winner but opposition parties accused the EPRDF of rigging the election and the EPRDF accused opposition parties of the same. The National Electoral Board was accused by the opposition of bias in the ways in which it handled the complaints and conducted the investigations. When the investigations were concluded, the opposition parties had won not less than 200 parliamentary seats. The problem arose when the main opposition party – Coalition for Unity Democracy (CUD [*Kinijit*]) – refused to accept the result. The CUD had legitimate policies relating to land rights, ethnic rights, national unity, electoral system, independence of the legislature and judiciary, etc. But some elements, particularly amongst the diaspora Ethiopians, who had directly or indirectly influenced the party, believed that although the opposition parties should be involved in the national elections, what they must focus on should be the *process* of the elections rather than the *results*. This, in their view, would make it possible for the opposition to claim that the elections were rigged and fraudulent and then instigate popular struggle, which would eventually bring down the EPRDF government.

The CUD then claimed that it won the polls, boycotted the parliament and refused to assume the administration of the city of Addis Ababa, where it had enjoyed a landslide victory. The party leadership decided to choose such a path claiming, rather incredibly, that the people urged them to do so. The CUD then encouraged the people to protest against the poll results. In November 2005, protesters took to the streets of Addis Ababa, blocked the roads and burned tires, and then engaged in confrontation with the police and security forces with ugly outcomes. Over 200 people were reported dead, and many were injured. Opposition leaders of the CUD, civil society workers and journalists were incarcerated. Treason and genocide charges were brought against them. Of course, both the grounds for jailing and the charges brought against them were politically motivated. Mounting pressure from Ethiopians and the international community forced Meles Zenawi's government to release the opposition politicians.

But opportunities, albeit limited, to use political processes to bring about change were squandered. Had the CUD taken the parliamentary seats and assumed the administration of Addis Ababa, the political landscape of the country would have changed significantly. As a result of the historic mistakes made in 2005 by both the ruling party and the CUD in particular, almost all the outcomes of the democratization efforts in the preceding years were wiped out. The EPRDF became much more repressive than before. Subsequent elections in 2010 and 2015 were not free, fair or transparent. While the opposition won one seat in the 2010 election, the EPRDF claimed to have won all parliamentary seats in the 2015 election. But both elections were hugely rigged, and therefore, many struggled to view the parliament and the executive branch as legitimate. Again the people of Ethiopia turned their backs on the EPRDF, which finally brought its demise after 27 years of rule.

One lesson we can learn from the last 90 years is that while a government that uses and abuses people, treats people with contempt and attempts to hang onto power through corrupt and illegitimate means or repressive policies may survive for 17, 27 or 44 years, its eventual demise is certain. Another lesson is that we should accept even in some testing circumstances that tolerance of dissenting views is a hallmark of democracy, while maintaining firmness in matters of principles and ensuring that freedom is subject to the rule of law. Furthermore, from the ways in which the Monarchy, Dergue and EPRDF ended, future governments should learn that there is no better way than respecting the freedom of the will of the people rather than suppressing it. Nor is there any better way than fighting any political cause through peaceful, parliamentary and democratic means. As Winston Churchill said in his speech in 1947: "Many forms of government have been tried, and will be tried in this world of sin and woe. No one pretends that democracy is perfect or all-wise. Indeed, it has been said that democracy is the worst form of government except for all those other forms that have been tried from time to time." Democracy has limitations, but it is not optional for Ethiopia. And our hope is that all its characteristics, namely elected representatives; free, fair and frequent elections; freedom of expression; autonomous associations; inclusive citizenship; and access to alternative, independent sources of information, will become a culture.

PRESENT AND FUTURE ELECTIONS

Ethiopia will hold its national elections in June 2021. I am painfully aware that Ethiopia's deep-seated problems are not going to be solved by one peaceful and democratic election or even two elections. Barak Obama says in his memoir, *A Promised Land*, that "no single election will settle" all the complex racial and economic issues in the U.S. Given that the U.S. is the biggest exporter of democracy to the world, it is going to take many elections to address Ethiopia's complex ethnic, political and economic issues. I believe, however, that Ethiopians currently have an opportunity despite the COVID-19 pandemic and worrying political and security developments in recent months. There exist dozens of active political parties with complex political fault lines.

For example, first, there are separatist forces within Oromia, who, through a strong support by Oromo diaspora groups, wish to create a separate state of Oromia. Second, there are political forces who wish to defend the current emphasis on ethnic-based administrative arrangements and maintain the existing constitutional provision, where regional states are sovereign and Ethiopia's sovereignty depends on the will of those sovereign regional states. Third, there are still others, who advocate the principle of citizenship and national sovereignty, and want to reverse the constitutional provision for ethnic federalism and replace it with a federalist system that is arranged along ethnic lines. Fourth, there are political forces who seek to maintain the current ethno-federalist political arrangements while putting a strong emphasis on the integrity of Ethiopia as a nation-state and the constitutional emphasis on strengthening the unity of nations, nationalities and peoples of Ethiopia as a single economic and political community. As Ethiopians go into the 2021 elections, these political fault lines will face them. I hope that many of the parties will focus on urgently pressing issues facing Ethiopia rather than appealing to ethnic loyalties.

Ethnic psychology is a fact of life. Ethnic loyalties run deeply in human beings and it is wrong to simply disavow ethnic reality. But transformed political leaders accept that ethnic loyalties take second place to a more fundamental understanding of being human. They submit to values and standards of conduct, where ethnic identity and all other identities are shaped and guided by our common humanity, which transcends all other identities. They keep the balance between individual rights and responsibilities and communal and relational rights and responsibilities. This keeps them from privileging ethnic loyalties over against shared identity and national unity and vice versa.

This means that transformed political leaders will be committed to Ethiopian-ness and treat Ethiopia as one sovereign nation-state of diverse people groups. Ethiopian-ness is a unifying story that is shared by more than 80 people groups who have happened or chosen to live on a piece of land and share God-given resources together. These groups also voluntarily share common values, common cultural heritage and expressions and uniting symbols. The vast majority of them have come to recognize and love this country called Ethiopia. What they actually love is not only that geographically determined land or incorporeal and intangible political construct called Ethiopia. What they love are those women and men whose lives and historical destinies are tied up with that of a political and geographical state called Ethiopia. Shared narrative has resulted in shared identity. Political leaders who are unable to accept this reality cannot bring about fairness, justice and peace in Ethiopia. They may even destroy both the unity of diverse people groups and the diversity of united people groups.

6

CHRISTIAN FAITH IN THE PUBLIC SQUARE

In the post-EPRDF Ethiopia, the questions as to how the sacred can relate to the religious and how religious arguments can play a role in the public square must be addressed. Karl Barth, a 20th century Christian theologian, said that a Christian should hold the Bible in one hand and the newspaper in the other, but always interpret the newspaper by the Bible. I would add here that an Ethiopian Christian politician should hold the Bible in one hand and the Ethiopian Constitution in the other, but interpret the Constitution by the Bible. This means that Ethiopia's supreme law and political standards should be measured by Scriptural principles.

This also means that while Christians are at once heavenly and earthly citizens, they should not dichotomize sharply between heavenly matters and earthly matters. As believers and citizens, Christians share in the privileges and responsibilities of membership of both church and society. As Lamin Sanneh argued in the *Accra Charter of Freedom and Citizenship*, in their dual citizenship, obedience to God requires Christians to promote works of civic righteousness in the earthly realm. "Believers are required to be productive and loyal citizens as a matter of principle, not just for personal political gain, and that example of moral citizenship constitutes an asset for good governance."

Christians are subject to the rule of God in their lives as believers. Accordingly, the privileges and obligations of *their faith* and *their citizenship* can foster democratic values in Ethiopia. Indeed, when citizenship is nurtured by properly understood and practiced Christian faith, and if the Church is enabled to continue to be a place where minds and lives are changed to change the world of politics and economics through moral teachings and example, Ethiopia will enjoy peace, security, unity, and prosperity.

However, there are still many in Ethiopia who would sharply distinguish between communities that exist by license of sacred power (religion) and political communities that exist by license of people power (politics). In their view, loyalty to Christian faith is a matter of private preference and cannot stand alongside loyalty to our state. This is consistent with the dictum *haymanot yegil hager yegara* (religion is a private matter; country belongs to everyone), which was often attributed to former Emperor, Haile-Silassie I. The EPRDF government cunningly and ruthlessly employed this dictum to prevent religion from playing a greater role in the public square. Politicians often quoted Article 11 of the Ethiopian Constitution, which states the separation of religion and state, to dismiss any suggestion otherwise.

Why did the EPRDF politicians attempt to make religious arguments vanish from the public square altogether? It was because they believed that the Ethiopian state could work without any contribution by religious groups, including the Christian Church. They failed to understand that the government functions within limits and does not monopolize the public square. It took them many years to realize that government functions within limits.

But the main reason for the formulators of the EPRDF ideology not allowing faith to play a role in the public square was because they were heavily influenced by Marxist philosophy, which underpinned almost all of their decisions and actions. They made no distinction between religious arguments and religious dogmatism, so they allowed no religious argument in the public square. After the EPRDF took over the country in 1991, many whose values were shaped by Christian ideals joined them. All of them tried to sing from the same hymn sheet as that of the original founders of the EPRDF.

In this process, Christian politicians made their faith a private matter and engaged in a zero-sum political game, as is the case in Marxism-Leninism. The disconnect between what underpinned their values (Christianity) and the political values (Revolutionary Democracy) was palpable for critical eyes. As a result, many of those Christians who joined the EPRDF and sought to adopt its ideological values in its fullness could not come across as authentic. Whether religious or not, no political leader can be seen as authentic if they do not state what influences what they say, where they come from and what shapes their moral fiber.

In the post-EPRDF Ethiopia, I hope that Christian politicians speak about values that matter most to them and, in so doing, bring a complete version of themselves to the public square. The former British Prime Minister Gordon Brown, in his political memoir, says:

> If the values that matter most to me are the values that I speak about least, then I am, at least in part, in denial of who I really am. This was, to my regret, a problem that I never really resolved. I suspect I was thought of more like a technician lacking solid convictions. And despite my strong personal religious beliefs, I never really countered that impression. Instead of defining myself, I gave my opponents room to define me.[1]

Gordon Brown grew up as a Christian. His father was a church minister, who lived in a poverty stricken part of Scotland. He taught him to treat everyone equally. He also taught him that he should never be subservient or condescending to anyone. Brown says his father's ministry was woven into his life. His father's influence and his powerful sermons remained pivotal throughout his political life. Christianity shaped his values.

It is these Christian values that Brown spoke about least during his political life. I hope Christians in the public square in Ethiopia would not deny who they really are and their primary accountability to God. Having said this, while Christians in the public square are primarily accountable to God and the Jesus law, they should never think that theocracy overrules democracy. As Abraham Lincoln famously said, Christian politicians should not claim that God is on their side, but they should hope that they are on God's side or, I would add, they should have a clear conviction that they are on God's side.

Then, their example of moral citizenship and leadership in the public square will promote good governance.

For this to be achieved in the post-EPRDF Ethiopia, however, the questions as to how the sacred can relate to the religious and how religious arguments can play a role in the public square must be addressed in a manner that is balanced and objective. Admittedly, a state under constitutional democracy cannot be run through claims of words of knowledge or theological dogmatism. But religious arguments in the public sphere are different from theological dogmatism. Religious arguments enable public debate in order for us to reach agreement on what is good for society, what facilitates societal moral progress, what allows us to address societal ills such as poverty, ignorance and inter-ethnic conflicts, and what reinforces peaceful co-existence.

A democratic state is not truly democratic if it has no room for engagement between believers and non-believers. Democratic citizens are not truly democratic if they are not able or willing to openly engage with one another. This includes religious citizens engaging with secular citizens by using a language that is free from theological dogmatism and generally accessible to the public. This is the time in Ethiopia to agree on the proper place religious arguments should have in the public square. Any society is impoverished if its public square is emptied of religious discourse that centers on truth, generosity of spirit, trust, civic righteousness and mutual obligations to one another's welfare. In short, hope for Ethiopia lies in religious discourse having a place in the public square and secular citizens and religious citizens engaging with each other.

I have tried to argue, albeit very briefly, that it takes so many things for Ethiopia to see true socio-cultural and political transformation. For example, it takes reconditioned social capital, renewed perspective on religion, reformed stance on gender issues, revolutionized education, restored relationships and transformed minds and lives, revitalized moral agents and redesigned statecraft. I have also argued that Ethiopia's hope lies in it remaining a secular but not secularized state, holding a successful free, fair and transparent election and Christians playing a greater role in the public square. Most important of all, I would like to finish my discussion by expressing this: Ethiopia's hope lies in its citizens' uncompromising determination to build a civilization of love.

Ethiopia is now referred to as a family of nations, nationalities and peoples, which should be bound up primarily by love and then by a constitution. Where love reigns supreme, freedom abounds. Where it does not, fear, which darkens human existence, abounds. What Ethiopia needs is "a common effort to build the civilization of love, founded on the universal values of peace, solidarity, justice and liberty." The heart of this civilization is freedom of individuals and communities "lived in self-giving solidarity and responsibility."[2] The civilization of love is different from utilitarian civilization. The latter treats a person primarily as a productive instrument and promotes self-centered individualism and an ethos of happiness characterized by immediate gratification. On the contrary, the civilization of love works for the common good and is characterized by a demanding act of self-giving.[3] Ethiopia's hope lies in politics adopting the concept of the civilization of love. The Church (*ekklesia*), as a body that promotes the civilization of love, can play a role in helping politics to center itself in love, forgiveness and peace.

❧ 7 ❧

CONCLUDING REMARKS

In this book, I have tried to argue, albeit briefly, that Ethiopia's hope for a better future lies in its transformed women and men and a deep understanding and fundamental recalibration of a complex web of historical, socio-political, cultural, religious and moral factors. Anyone, who has the audacity to believe and hope that there are better days ahead for Ethiopia and seeks to contribute towards the materialization of that belief and hope, must accept the complexity of these factors. One must also assume that any approach to addressing Ethiopia's problems is fraught with complications and ambiguities.

The main reason for this is because Ethiopia's problems are historically bound up with one another, like its 80 people groups, whose historical destinies are irreversibly bound up with one another's. So, addressing one problem or one people group's source of grievances alone will not solve Ethiopia's problems. For example, addressing economic issues in the north without addressing political issues in the south, or socio-cultural issues in the west, or religious issues in the east, cannot bring about peace, prosperity and security for Ethiopia as a whole. Ethiopia's historical tragedies and successes are like a pack of cards. Each card is propped up by its neighbor, which props up another card in its turn and so on. When one card collapses and falls, then the whole pack steadily goes down.

I, like many Ethiopians, have witnessed over the last 50 years how focusing on a single issue such as class (e.g., feudalism, capitalism) or ethnicity has not solved Ethiopia's troubles. Nor has magnifying one people group's past grievances by denying or overlooking collective wounds. Indeed, simplified, isolated and ethnographically determined approaches to address Ethiopia's problems have left the country and its citizens with more problems. Ethiopia's survival and flourishing as a nation, in my view, is dependent on each person and each people group propping up *the other*.

It is with this in mind that I have argued in this book that to realize Ethiopia's hope and to provide the next generation with a better future, it takes courage and determination from us Ethiopians to be self-critical and relook at the way we think, do things and relate to one another. In my view, Ethiopia's hope lies in reconditioned social capital, a renewed perspective on religion, a reformed stance on gender issues, revolutionized education, restored relationships, transformed minds and lives, revitalized moral agents and redesigned statecraft. I have also argued that Ethiopia's hope lies in the nation remaining a secular but not secularized state, developing a culture of holding successful free, fair and transparent elections, and Christians playing a more significant role in the public square.

I am acutely aware that there is a lot more that can be said in connection with this; that I have not included issues such as the environment, macroeconomics, geopolitics and international partnerships; and that I have discussed issues briefly and, therefore, inexorably incompletely. However, this book is meant to be a brief introduction to a non-Ethiopian audience, which, I hope, will also be of some value to Ethiopian readers. In conclusion, I echo the words of one Jewish writer, who wrote a book about a hundred years before Christ and concluded it by saying: "If it is well told and to the point, that is what I myself desired; if it is poorly done and mediocre, that was the best I could do."

NOTES

INTRODUCTION

1. See, for example, Richard Pankhurst, *The History of Famine and Epidemics in Ethiopia Prior to the Twentieth Century*, Addis Ababa, 1985; *Economic History of Ethiopia 1800-1935*, Addis Ababa, 1968; Peter Cotterell, *Cry Ethiopia*, UK: MARC/Kingsway Publications, 1988.
2. Cotterell, *Cry Ethiopia*, 149-159.

3. HOPE FOR ETHIOPIA

1. Donald Levine, *Greater Ethiopia: The Evolution of a Multiethnic Society*, Chicago: University of Chicago Press (2nd ed), 2000, 119-120.
2. Lamin Sanneh, Unpublished Paper on Religion, Ethnicity and Politics, Nairobi Conference, 2018.
3. J.S. Trimingham, *Islam in Ethiopia*, London, 1952.
4. See, for example, Travis Owens, "Beleaguered Muslim Fortresses and Ethiopian Imperial Expansion from 13th to 16th Century", Naval Post Graduate School, California, 2008, 1ff; Manuel Ramos, "From Beleaguered Fortress to Belligerent Cities in Ethiopia", *State and Societal Challenges in the Horn of Africa: Conflict and Processes of State Formation, Reconfiguration and Disintegration*, Center of African Studies, University Institute of Lisbon, 14-31.
5. Haghai Erlich, *Ethiopia and the Middle East*, London: Lynne Rienner Publishers, 1995, 6.
6. Erlich, *Ethiopia*, 9-10.
7. "I invite you also to follow me and believe in the God who hath sent me. I am His Messenger. I am His Messenger. I invite you and your armies to join the Faith of the Almighty God. I have delivered to you the Message of God, made clear to you the meaning of the Message. I have done so in all sincerity and I trust you will value the sincerity, which has prompted this message. He who obeys the guidance of God becomes heir to the blessings of God (Zurkani.)" Hazrat Mizra Bashiruddin Mahmud Ahmad, *Life of Muhammad*, 209.
8. *Life of Muhammad*, 209-210; Erlich, *Ethiopia*, 9.

9. Erlich, *Ethiopia,* 9.
10. When the Ottomans were controlling Massawa, in 1647 Emperor Fasilidas entered into agreement with the Ottomans to stop the Jesuits from entering Ethiopia. See also Erlich, *Ethiopia,* 37.
11. Erlich, *Ethiopia,* 9-11.
12. The Ethiopian king who attempted was called Abraha, who was ruling South Arabia at the time. His campaign – recorded in the Quran – ended in defeat and disaster, later turning Abraha a mythical figure of evil in Islamic tradition. See David W. Phillipson, Foundations of an African Civilisation: Aksum and the northern Horn, 1000 BC - AD 1300 (Eastern Africa Series), Melton, Woodbridge, UK: James Currey, 2012, 205-206; John Binns, *The Orthodox Church of Ethiopia*: A History, London: Bloomsbury, 2016, 125.
13. Erlich, *Ethiopia,* 10-19, 21-25.
14. See Phillipson, *Foundations*, 208-237.
15. Phillipson, *Foundations*, 228-229.
16. See Ulrich Brauckaemper, *Islamic History and Culture in Southern Ethiopia.*, Collected Essays, Goettinger Studien zur Ethnologie, Band 9, Muenster, Berlin, 2004. Erlich, *Ethiopia,* 12.
17. See Erlich, *Ethiopia,* 24.
18. See also Owens, 'Beleaguered', 20ff.
19. Erlich, *Ethiopia,* 27.
20. Owens, 'Beleaguered', 25-31.
21. Erlich, *Ethiopia,* 30.
22. Erlich, *Ethiopia,* 31.
23. See also Erlich, *Ethiopia,* 42-43.
24. Erlich, *Ethiopia,* 42.
25. See, for example, Erlich, *Ethiopia,* 51.
26. Erlich, *Ethiopia,* 62-63.
27. Asfa-Wossen Asrate (translated by Peter Lewis), *King of Kings: The Triumph and Tragedy of Emperor Haile-Selassie I of Ethiopia*, London: Haus Publishing Limited, 24.
28. Asfa-Wossen, *King of Kings*, 27.
29. See, for example, Mustafa Kabha and Haggai Erlich, 'Al-Ahbash and Wahhabiyya: Interpretations of Islam', *International Journal of Middle East Studies*, Vol 38:4 (2006), 519-538.
30. Lamin Sanneh, "Sovereignty and Civil Society: Comparative African Perspective on *Ecclesia* and *Ummah*," unpublished paper, June 2017.
31. Asfa-Wossen Asrate, *King of Kings*, 24.
32. Lamin Sanneh, *Beyond Jihad*, 241.
33. Sanneh, *Beyond Jihad: The Pacifist Tradition in West African Islam*, USA: Oxford University Press, 2016, 240.

34. Sanneh, *Beyond Jihad*, 250.

35. Emmanuel Todd, *Who is Charlie?: Zenophobia and the New Middle Class* (translated by Andrew Brown), Polity, 2015.

36. Bryan Wilson, *Magic and the Millennium: A Sociological Study of Religious Church Movements of Protest Among Tribal and Third-World Peoples*, London: Paladin, 1973.

37. See, for example, Wilson, *Magic*, 23-26.

38. Getachew Haile, 'The Missionary's Dream: An Ethiopian Perspective on Western Missions in Ethiopia' in Aasulv Lande, Samuel Rubenson and Getachew Haile (eds), *The Missionary Factor in Ethiopia: Papers from a Symposium on the Impact of European Missions on Ethiopian Society, Lund University, August 1996 (Studies in the Intercultural History of Christianity)*, 3.

39. Lamin Sanneh, Unpublished Paper on 'Ethnicity, Morality and the Public Square in Kenya', 2018.

40. For example, A. Giddens, *Beyond Left and Right: The Future of Radical Politics*, Stanford University Press, 1994; *The Third Way: The Renewal of Social Democracy*, Polity Press, 2001.

41. See, for example, Yonatan Tesfaye Fessha, *Ethnic Diversity and Federalism: Constitution Making in South Africa and Ethiopia*, London and New York, Routledge, 182-183.

42. Kwame Anthony Appiah, "Mistaken Identities: Creed, Country, Color, Culture" Reith Lectures, 2016 – https://fridayroom.files.wordpress.com/2017/01/2016_reith1-4_appiah_mistaken_identies.pdf.

43. I am indebted to Kwame Appiah for the term *cosmopolitan patriot*. I have added 'ethno' because of the reality of ethnic identity in our context. Appiah does not deny the necessity of nation and nationalism, but he argues that being a citizen of a nation state should not necessarily clash with being a citizen of the world. I agree with him.

4. SECULAR STATE VERSUS SECULARIST STATE

1. Lamin Sanneh, "Christianity, Politics, and Citizenship with Reference to Africa: A Comparative Inquiry," unpublished lecture, Accra, Ghana 2010.

2. Sanneh, Lamin. "Sovereignty and Civil Society: Comparative African Perspective on Ecclesia and Ummah," unpublished lecture.

5. DEMOCRATIC ELECTIONS IN ETHIOPIA

1. See an English translation by Sir E. A. Wallis Budge, *The Queen of Sheba and Her Only Son Menyelek (Kebra Negest)*, Cambridge, Ontario, 2000.

6. CHRISTIAN FAITH IN THE PUBLIC SQUARE

1. *My Life, Our Times*, The Bodley Head, London, 2017, 429.
2. See Chester Gillis [editor], *Political Papacy: John Paul II, Benedict XVI, and Their Influence*, Routledge, 2016, 81.
3. Gillis, Papacy, 82.

ABOUT THE AUTHOR

Desta Heliso (PhD) served as lecturer and director of the Ethiopian Graduate School of Theology (EGST) in Addis Ababa. He also served on the Board of the Inter-Religious Council of Ethiopia. He currently resides in London but continues to coordinate the Centre for Ancient Christianity and Ethiopian Studies at EGST in Addis Ababa. He is also a fellow of the Center for Early African Christianity (New Haven) and a visiting lecturer at the London School of Theology (London).

CPSIA information can be obtained
at www.ICGtesting.com
Printed in the USA
FSHW020835111021
85267FS

9 781624 280160